Contents

Glossary   **161**

MUHAMMAD MOJLUM KHAN

ADAPTED BY

IMRAN MOGRA

YOUNG ADULT EDITION

THE MUSLIM 100

VOL.2

The Lives, Thoughts and Achievements of The Most Influential Muslims In History

The Muslim 100 YA Edition:
The Lives, thoughts and achievements of the
most influential Muslims in History.
Volume 2

First published by Kube Publishing Ltd,
Markfield Conference Centre
Ratby Lane, Markfield,
Leicestershire LE67 9SY

United Kingdom
Tel: +44 (0) 1530 249230
Website: www.kubepublishing.com
Email: info@kubepublishing.com

British Library Cataloguing-in-Publication Data

ISBN 978-1-84774-264-3 Paperback

ISBN 978-1-84774-265-0 Ebook

Cover Design: Amaan Ansari
Typesetting: LiteBook Prepress Services

Calligraphy: M. Swallay Mungly

Introduction

It goes without saying that societies across the world are experiencing changes at a very fast pace. We are living at a time when the world is interconnected, and instant communication has become normal. People who were once at the far corners of the world have virtually been brought together and can communicate immediately, perhaps to know one another better. One of the questions that this book invites you to think about is the extent to which you are aware of and connected to the history of Islam and Muslims. Are you a stranger to these great people who have left everlasting legacies for humanity?

Many educators, both Muslims and others, have realised the need to highlight and celebrate the huge contributions that Muslims have made over the centuries in the development of different subjects which gave the world the knowledge and means to improve life and civilisation. It is important for you to recognise that much of this history was deliberately suppressed, degraded, and doubted. Have you wondered why? In fact, there was a time when such history was absent "even among some universities and school syllabuses in may countries" You might want to ponder as to why this significant aspect of Muslim heritage and history of humanity was 'hidden'.

One the reasons may well be that it served the purposes of the powerful who wanted to keep their imperialist strategies and colonisation mission alive. Part of this mission involved the creation of a Muslim mind which felt inferior about itself and devalued its own knowledge, people, heritage, and lifestyle. Looking forward, this trend needs to be reversed, and Muslims need to take their rightful place on the world stage. Muslims and Islam matter. Therefore, it is my sincere hope that educational institutions will include this book in their libraries or as part of the syllabuses to enlighten their learners and to keep Islam's legacy alive.

The contribution of Muslims, as you will read, is a vast field and much has been written about it. Some of it remains in the Arabic language in libraries and in personal collections to be discovered by others and presented to the world. A lot of it has been ruined and continues to be destroyed through neglect, natural loss, modernisation, and wars.

In this book, you will find the fantastic contributions of Muslim scholars to literature, calligraphy, political administration, history, sociology, theology, finance and economy, philosophy, science, architecture, Hadith, *tafsir*, *aqidah*, music, education, morality, mathematics, astronomy, medicine, chemistry, travel, logic, faith and spirituality. You will marvel at the physical geography of forts, palaces, mosques, mausoleums and libraries. You will also reflect upon some pleasant as well as unpleasant events and behaviours of individuals. This past will offer insights into what happened in previous centuries. As a historian, you will interpret the past for the benefit of the present and future.

You will be surprised with the interesting information about Muslim centres of learning which flourished in Europe, North Africa, the Middle East and Asia. You will come across some of the amazing libraries in Cordoba, Spain, established by generous patrons, which contained hundreds of thousands of books accessible to all. You are about to open the pages of the profiles of kings, saints, nobles, tyrants and people with questionable actions, morals and beliefs.

It has been said that history is a mirror of the people, and it is through this mirror of history that people see themselves and the performance of past peoples. As you turn the pages in this collection, you will encounter the photographic memory that some people had. For example, the compilers of Hadith literature memorised thousands of sayings of the Prophet Muhammad (ﷺ) and saved them for future generations. Muslims are forever indebted to them for preserving the lifestyle of the Prophet (ﷺ) for everyone. These narratives inform you about Muslim heritage so that you become conscious of your connections with your predecessors and hopefully give you a sense of direction for your life ahead.

Whilst you curiously examine these biographies, take note of the social history of the time and think about the trade links, commerce, travels, the lifestyle and other social characteristics of these historical periods. There are fascinating gems of information both in terms of facts and figures. Try to learn and remember some of these and share them with others. But you must see beyond these facts and probe into the cause and effects of the rise and fall of nations and their rulers.

Spirituality is a theme that runs through most of the lives of these remarkable people. In whatever they pursued, they did not ignore this critical aspect of their life, their relationship with Allah and their pursuit of achieving higher ideals in life. They always kept, in their mind and heart, the Hereafter as their final destination and prepared for it diligently. But they were not only concerned about themselves. They wished others to be mindful of Allah, to become better people and live in kindness with a view to eternal happiness. How did they achieve this?

These brilliant narratives will illustrate to you the preservation, reformation, revival and propagation of Islam and the different methodologies adopted by scholars, saints, activists, politicians, philanthropists, Imams, shaykhs and soldiers for this. They preserved the light of Islam in a variety of ways. They aimed to beautify (*ihsan*) characters, ethics and manners. They also aimed to purify (*tazkiya*) the heart and soul. They taught (*ta'lim*) knowledge. They converted and disseminated (*da'wah*) the message of Islam.

One of the most fascinating observations to make is that there is a universal characteristic that flows through these people as they belonged to different cultures, races, ethnicities and languages and that they were were rich and poor, male and female. Actually, some were crippled, like Tamerlane, who was one of the world's greatest conquerors, and others were orphaned very young. Yet they achieved great accomplishments. Mothers have been the bedrock for the likes of Imam al-Bukhari and many others, as you will read.

As you study these short biographies, you will notice their sincerity, determination and humility in search of learning. This enabled them to travel to distant lands and sit at the feet of experts with different faiths, cultures and worldviews. In doing so, they learnt other local languages, translated books and critically evaluated other people's knowledge and truth claims. They then made this knowledge widely accessible.

You will also be exposed to some Muslim, Greek and other philosophical thoughts which may appear unfamiliar to you. As you read, you will understand that some of these civilisations are different from the Islamic civilisation, spirituality and morality. However, some understanding of this is necessary, without making generalisations about Western thought and modernism, because these ideals and ideas continue to influence the political, social, ethical, aesthetic and economical thought of the current modern world. You will also encounter the different thoughts and schools that exists among Muslims.

You will recognise that unity and justice were cornerstones for many of those leaders who were more successful in providing stability and security. These then facilitated the establishment of educational centres, hospitals and general public order. Once these were functioning and secure, the wellbeing and prosperity of their peoples and societies followed. On the other hand, exploitation, oppression, greed, nepotism, corruption, deception and disunity brought downfall. In other words, be curious as you dive into the past and arrive at an appreciation about the how and why of events.

You are living at a time when Western civilization and the powers associated with them are at the top. Muslim nations are weaker and controlled but Muslims have spiritual strength. This book will make you realise that the story of Muslims was once different and the direction that the world is taking can be changed. You need to take up this challenge to your heart to lead the world. "There is plenty to inspire you and for you to aspire to."

As you have a dialogue with this historical period, I sincerely hope that what you learn from this collection creates a love for further knowledge. I hope you will appreciate their amazing achievements and that their legacy motivates you to greatness and the service of humanity. Nobody ever imagined that Islam, which was on verge of extinction during the night of *hijra,* would spread to all corners of the world and become a religion with over a billion followers. You are about to discover how that happened.

The biographies have been presented in a chronological order. It will help you to place the geography, personalities and events in a systematic order of history. From the school and curriculum perspective to grasp history well, an understanding of its chronology is important. The chronology will support you to develop a better mental framework of the past so that you have a secure grasp of the timeline of Islam as it has unfolded over the centuries. You should also be able to extend and deepen your knowledge and understanding of local and world history. This will provide you with a well-informed context for learning history in general. Register in your mind the younger age at which some of them died but how massive their success and impact has been. Overall, you will identify significant events, make connections, compare and contrast and analyse trends over centuries.

Imran Mogra
July 2025

27

Jabir ibn Hayyan
(b.cir.738 - d.813 CE) /
(b.121 - d.198 AH)

Chemistry is concerned with the composition of matter (gas, liquid or solid) and of the changes taking place in them under certain conditions. Along with physics and biology, it is one of the three major physical sciences. As in physics and biology, the Muslim contribution to the development of chemistry was both great and unprecedented. Indeed, the origin of the word 'chemistry' can be traced to its Arabic root *al-kimiya,* which was also translated as alchemy. Perhaps the word *al-kimiya* originated from the Egyptian *khem*, meaning 'black'; both the ancient Egyptians and Greeks considered chemistry to be the 'art of *khem*'.

As such, they sought to discover the mysteries which surrounded the practice of this 'black art', especially the transformation of base metal into solid gold or silver, probably for economic reasons. Among the early Muslim practitioners of alchemy were Khalid ibn Yazid, the grandson of Caliph Mu'awiyah, and Ja'far al-Sadiq (see chapter 22), the well-known Islamic scholar of Madinah who acquired knowledge of this subject from a combination of religious and Syriac sources.

However, their understanding of chemistry was only limited to fusion, distillation and fabrication of certain chemical substances to produce desirable products, without undermining their spiritual dimension. Rather, the early Muslim chemists considered alchemy – in its highest form – to be a spiritual science, thus capable of purifying and liberating the human spirit without undermining the physical dimension of those chemical substances. This situation continued until Jabir ibn Hayyan, known in the Latin West as Geber, emerged to open the way for the emergence of alchemy as an independent branch of science.

Jabir ibn Hayyan al-Kufi al-Sufi was born in Tus in the Persian province of Khurasan. He originated from the southern Arabian tribe of Azd; his ancestors moved to Kufah during the early years of Islamic expansion. His father was a well-known druggist who supported the Abbasids in their political campaign against their Umayyad rivals. While Jabir was a child, his father was captured and sentenced to death by the Umayyad judiciary for supporting politically rebellious activities.

After his father's execution, Jabir and his family rapidly fell into poverty, leaving his mother with no alternative except to send her son to Arabia to continue his education there. He studied Arabic language, literature and traditional Islamic sciences before receiving advanced training in Islamic sciences, spirituality and alchemy under the guidance of Ja'far al-Sadiq, who was, at the time, one of the Muslim world's most renowned experts on Islamic sciences and spirituality. Thereafter, he studied astronomy, astrology, cosmology and further aspects of medicine and alchemy.

Blessed with a sharp intellect and an inquisitive mind, Jabir was admired by all his tutors for his total devotion and dedication to his studies. As a practising Sufi, he was also in the habit of going to spiritual retreats. His understanding of *Sufism* (spiritualitly) was far from being other-worldly, as he found time to learn and master the experimental sciences too. As a follower of the Sufi *tariqa* (Order) founded by Abul Hashim of Kufah, Jabir successfully combined spiritualism with physical and intellectual activism. This in itself was a very rare achievement considering that the pursuit of both spirituality and worldly knowledge was not considered to be achievable at the time.

Nevertheless, after completing his formal education in the empirical sciences, he became a successful medical practitioner and his reputation soon began to spread far and wide. When Harun al-Rashid, the celebrated Abbasid Caliph, heard about Jabir, he recruited him to his research centre in Baghdad. The ruling Abbasid elites were known for promoting learning and higher education and they encouraged Muslim scholars, philosophers and scientists to come to Baghdad and do their research in all branches of science. Jabir thus became associated with the Abbasids, especially the Barmakids who at the time served as chief advisors to the Caliph. Thanks to the Abbasids' generosity, his dreadful economic situation improved, enabling him to pursue research in the experimental sciences, especially in alchemy.

Although Jabir continued to live in Kufah, he travelled regularly to Baghdad to collaborate with the leading Muslim scholars and scientists of the day. As a scientist, he was interested in both theoretical as well as experimental science. Indeed, he loved learning and scholarship so much that he became thoroughly familiar with a wide range of subjects including *kalam* (theology), Sufism, astrology, cosmology, medicine and music. However, it was in the field of alchemy, or chemistry, that he made his lasting contribution. In addition to studying ancient Egyptian and Greek alchemy, Jabir acquired a profound knowledge and understanding of traditional Islamic sciences. This enabled him to develop a fresh method to study alchemy. Before his own time, alchemy was widely considered to be a spiritual rather than an experimental science, but after Jabir, it became an experimental science, detached from its spiritual roots.

Although Jabir was the pioneer of experimental alchemy, he did not fail to highlight the spiritual features of alchemy. By doing this, he tried to maintain the continuity between a purely spiritual, as opposed to a thoroughly experimental, alchemy. Nonetheless, his promotion of experimental alchemy did represent a significant break with the past. It was a positive step forward in the advancement of chemistry as we know it today. Had it not been for Jabir's bold and innovative experimental scientific method, the development of chemistry as a separate scientific discipline would no doubt have been delayed by at least a few centuries, if not longer.

Jabir may not have been the first Muslim to study alchemy, but he was certainly one of the first to engage in experimental alchemy. For this reason, today he is widely considered to be the 'Father of Islamic Alchemy' and one of the creators of chemistry. For the first time in the history of chemistry, he founded a fully operational chemical laboratory, in his native Kufah. He devised and conducted a large number of chemical experiments to prove or reject his theoretical views on many chemical matters. By personally designing and carrying out live chemical experimentation in his private laboratory, he banished the ghosts of secrecy and superstition which had overshadowed alchemy. He elevated this important branch of learning to a level equivalent to that of astronomy, medicine and mathematics. This also prompted other Muslim and non-Muslim scientists to pursue further studies and research in chemical science. Jabir's experimental approach to alchemy, combined with the discovery of his private chemical laboratory in Kufah two centuries after his death, proved that he was a great alchemist and pioneering chemist.

Using his experimental approach to alchemy, Jabir named and classified chemicals and minerals into three broad categories. The first category consisted of spirits (such as sulphur, mercury, camphor and arsenic compounds) which, he argued, could be refined through the application of heat. The second category included metals like gold, silver, lead, tin, copper, iron and zinc. The final category consisted of pulverised substances, even though he pointed out that some pulverised elements, such as living creatures, were made of both spirit and matter. In his attempt to provide a scientific explanation of the composition of the body-spirit, he also highlighted the role and relationship between these two elements in the formation of a balanced living creature.

In the process, he devised an original scientific theory which came to be known as the 'Sulphur-Mercury Theory'. He not only conducted numerous chemical experiments to prove this theory, but also explained how chemists could propose theories about the nature of various chemicals or substances before carrying out practical experimentation to determine the validity of their theoretical proposals. Thus, Jabir did much more than develop an experimental method in his study of alchemy; he went further, by suggesting new techniques and procedures which could be utilised in chemical study and research.

Not surprisingly, he is today considered to be the pioneer of the chemical processes of distillation, filtration, crystallisation, sublimation, reaction and fixation which all students of chemistry take for granted as standard procedures in experimental chemistry. For the first time, he explained the chemical process which facilitated the preparation and purification of various mineral acids such as sulphuric, hydrochloric and nitric acids. By conducting extensive chemical experimentation in his laboratory, Jabir made several remarkable discoveries. For instance, by developing a special acidic powder, he was able to dissolve solid gold and produce a chemical substance which enabled him to separate gold from silver.

In addition to this, he discovered several other important chemicals including white lead, sulphur, silver and mercury compounds which are now used by commercial industries all over the world to produce household products like paint and washing powder. Likewise, he coined many technical terms such as *alkali*, *antimony*, *alembic* and *cinnabar* which have today become commonplace around the world. In short, his contribution to the development of science, especially experimental alchemy or chemistry, was nothing short of remarkable.

Like many other great medieval Muslim scholars and scientists, Jabir's motivation for pursuing scientific research was to develop a better understanding of humans and their environment, rather than seek personal glory or acquire material benefits. On the contrary, he led a very simple, pious and productive life, devoted entirely to the pursuit of knowledge. Given his close friendship with the Barmakids during the early years of Caliph Harun al-Rashid's reign, he had free access to all the royal libraries in Baghdad, but after the Barmakids fell from Abbasid grace, Jabir also lost his sponsorship. This prompted him to return home to Kufah where he continued his research in alchemy. Jabir died at the age of around seventy-five and was buried in Kufah.

He was not only an outstanding chemist, but he was also a great writer who authored more than one hundred books and treatises on aspects of alchemy, chemistry, cosmology, astrology, medicine, music and spirituality. Although al-Nadim, the celebrated bibliographer and author of *al-Fihrist*, recorded the names of some of his books and treatises, unfortunately, his list is not complete.

According to other historians, most of Jabir's books perished in 1258 CE during the Mongol sack of Baghdad. Given that the number of writings attributed to him was so large, some historians consider most of the books attributed to him as not exclusively written by him, but rather as written by a group of scholars who used his name to gain wider circulation and acceptance. However, the majority of historians have dismissed this view. They argue that as an all-round thinker, scientist and creative writer, he would have written prolifically just like al-Kindi (see chapter 35) and Ibn Sina (see chapter 52), both of whom were also great scientists and managed to author more than two hundred books and treatises each.

Inspired by Jabir's remarkable contribution to the field of alchemy and chemistry, other great Muslim scientists, like al-Kindi and Abu Bakr al-Razi (see chapter 39), pursued their research in these subjects. Likewise, after his works were translated into Latin and other European languages during the thirteenth and fourteenth centuries, Jabir's ideas had a profound impact on medieval European thinkers and scientists. The great Western thinkers like Albertus Magnus, also known as Albert the Great, and Roger Bacon used to fondly refer to him as that 'famous Arabian Prince and Philosopher'.

28

Harun al-Rashid
(b.766 - d.809 CE) / (b.149 - d.193 AH)

The Abbasid Empire was one of the foremost political dynasties to have ruled the Islamic world. The Umayyad era ended suddenly following the Abbasid revolution of 750 CE when Marwan II, the last Umayyad ruler, was defeated by the supporters of Abdullah ibn Muhammad (b. 721-d. 754 CE), otherwise known as Abul Abbas al-Saffah. After this, the Abbasids ruled the Muslim world until the Mongol armies emerged from Asia in the thirteenth century. Al-Saffah is generally considered to be the founder of the Abbasid Empire. But actually, it was his brother Abdullah ibn Muhammad (b. 754-d. 775 CE), better known as al-Mansur, who played a pivotal role in consolidating Abbasid rule. Al-Mansur was a shrewd and gifted ruler who was equally famous for his personal piety, religiousness and unusual political and diplomatic skills.

After the death of al-Saffah, al-Mansur swiftly established his authority as Caliph and also founded the city of Baghdad. He ensured that a smooth political transition took place after his reign. Thus, Muhammad ibn al-Mansur (b. 744-d. 785 CE), better known as al-Mahdi, succeeded his father, al-Mansur. Al-Mahdi ruled for a decade. He had seven sons including Musa and Harun. After al-Mahdi's death, his son Musa ascended the Abbasid throne, but his rule only lasted a year. He was succeeded by Prince Harun al-Rashid who went on to become one of the Muslim world's most famous and influential rulers.

Harun was born in the central Iranian city of Rayy and was the favourite son of his parents. At the time of his birth, his father, al-Mahdi, was the governor of the Eastern region of the Abbasid Empire and his beautiful Yemeni mother, Khayzuran, was his father's favourite wife. Like his mother, Harun was an attractive child who grew up under the watchful gaze of his parents within the governor's grand residence surrounded by much wealth and luxury. Educated in Arabic and Islamic sciences during his early years, Harun soon became well-known for his bravery, intelligence and loyalty to the Abbasid clan.

His grandfather, al-Mansur, and his father, al-Mahdi, were very fond of the people of Makkah and Madinah. When he visited the sacred cities, al-Mahdi showered the locals with money and gifts and took a keen interest in carrying out restoration works on the *Haram al-Sharif* (sacred mosque) in Makkah. As a youngster, Harun accompanied his father to Makkah and Madinah during the *hajj* season, and instantly fell in love with the people of the two sacred cities. Al-Mahdi's generosity won over the people of Arabia. This helped to consolidate his Caliphal authority across the Islamic world. Also, at this time, al-Mahdi took the opportunity to introduce young Harun to the people of Makkah and Madinah as his potential successor.

On their return to Baghdad, al-Mahdi handed over Harun's educational needs to Yahya al-Barmaki, his talented Persian political advisor and administrator. Yahya trained him with care, teaching him political strategy and civil administration, and prepared him for political leadership in the near future. Yahya influenced Harun's education and political thinking so greatly that Harun came to rely on him for both psychological and emotional support. As expected, Harun grew up to be a very able and competent young man. Indeed, he was barely fifteen when his knowledge of military strategy and tactics was put to a severe test.

Harun was appointed the commander of the Abbasid army in 780 CE. His orders were to go and neutralise the Byzantine forces which had become a persistent thorn for the Abbasid army. By nominating Harun to lead the Abbasid forces against the Byzantines, al-Mahdi selected his favourite son to succeed him as the Abbasid

Caliph. Harun's military campaign against the Byzantines was very successful and he gained first-hand experience in leading an army on the battlefield. During his time with the army, he established a good relationship with the generals who became very fond of the young prince. Two years later, Harun was commissioned to lead another large-scale military campaign against the Byzantines. Again he returned home triumphant, having surrounded the Greeks inside Constantinople before Empress Irene came out and pleaded for peace. This was a remarkable achievement for the sixteen-year-old Harun. His efforts earned him the title of *al-Rashid*, meaning 'the rightly guided one'.

Due to over-indulgence, the Muslim rulers of the time often tended to die unexpectedly whilst still in their prime age. This prompted al-Mahdi to officially nominate his successor to avoid a bitter political struggle after his death. He had trained his sons Musa and Harun for political leadership. He also ensured everyone pledged their loyalty to Musa as his successor. Young Harun was confirmed as Musa's successor. When al-Mahdi died, Harun was the governor of the Western region of the Abbasid Empire. This stretched from Tunisia to Anbar outside of Baghdad. Likewise, Yahya al-Barmaki, his mentor, was put in charge of the political and civil administration of this vast province. As the govenor, Harun was mainly a figurehead.

Musa, who took the title of al-Hadi, succeeded his father as Caliph, but his reign did not last long. Like his father, he died under mysterious circumstances barely a year after ascending the Abbasid throne. Historians have provided conflicting accounts about the circumstances which led to al-Mahdi's and al-Hadi's deaths. When rumours, speculation and gossip began to spread throughout Baghdad like wildfire (especially after the death of al-Hadi), Khayzuran, the mother of Harun, stepped forward and took matters into her own hands. She summoned her favourite son, who was next in line to ascend the Abbasid throne and installed him as the new Caliph.

Harun was only twenty-one at the time. The young Caliph appointed the aged Yahya al-Barmaki as his personal advisor and guide. This was the highest-ranking government post in the land. With Yahya to guide him through the massive task of administering both the internal and external affairs of the vast Abbasid Empire,

Harun soon established himself as the undisputed ruler of the Muslim world. As a loyal, committed and extremely experienced bureaucrat, Yahya enjoyed Harun's full support and confidence, so much so that the young Caliph used to fondly refer to him as his 'father'. However, it was Yahya's younger son, Ja'far, who forged a close friendship with the young Caliph. Like Harun, he was in his early twenties and was well-known for his love of glamour, fun and adventure. They had so much in common that Ja'far subsequently became famous as Harun's loyal companion in the world-famous adventure story *The One Thousand and One Nights* (*Alf Layla wa Layla* – also known as *The Arabian Nights*).

If Harun became famous as a glamorous and fun-loving Caliph, then he was equally well-known for his personal religiousness, piety and generosity. As a devout Muslim, he became the first and only Caliph to have performed the *hajj* no fewer than eight times with his beloved wife Zubaidah (chapter 29). Following in the footsteps of his father and grandfather, every time Harun visited Makkah and Madinah, he showered the locals with gifts of clothing and money. Before each *hajj* season, he took it upon himself to personally prepare for the journey. He also encouraged his officials as well as the masses to accompany him, leaving the affairs of the State in the safe hands of his Barmakid viziers and other high-ranking government officials.

During his reign as Caliph, he also radically reformed the civil and administrative systems of the State to increase efficiency and effectiveness across all levels of his government. To put an end to all Byzantine invasions, he started military campaigns against them. By doing this, he became the first ruler in Islamic history to have led the *hajj* delegation and an army onto the battlefield in the same year. Harun's greatness lay in the fact that he not only preached but also led his people by his personal example. This naturally made him very popular with his officials, as well as the public.

In fact, during his reign as Caliph, Harun sent military expeditions against the Byzantines every year. He was determined to undermine their plots. He utilised his profound knowledge and understanding of military strategy and tactics against the Byzantines with remarkable success. He often left the political and civil affairs of his government in the hands of the Barmakids so that he could focus his full attention on the external enemies of his empire. His rule represented the peak of Abbasid glory and achievement. After establishing political stability, increasing economic wealth, raising educational standards and promoting social peace and solidarity across the Islamic world, he founded the first fully operational hospital in Baghdad.

He also established a library and research centre, known as *Bait al-Hikmah* (the House of Wisdom), where Muslim scientists, mathematicians, astronomers and philosophers pursued pioneering studies and research in all the sciences of the day. Moreover, he was instrumental in the development of an effective postal system across the Abbasid Empire. He constructed new roads and highways to facilitate trade and commerce, as well as long-distance travel and communication between the different regions of his empire.

Under Harun's wise and inspirational leadership, a thriving and tolerant society emerged in the Muslim world, where scholars, writers and thinkers were able to engage in debate and discussion on religious, philosophical, scientific and literary themes without any fear of political, religious or social sanctions. For this reason, his reign became known as the Golden Age of Abbasid rule. The echoes of this period naturally found their way into the stories of the famous *One Thousand and One Nights*. Being the main hero of this epic tale, he is portrayed roaming around Baghdad, the magnificent city of palaces, populated by wealthy civil servants and middle-class merchants, engaging in hilarious adventures (often in the middle of the night), accompanied by his colleagues Ja'far the Barmakid and Abu Nuwas, the well-known poet and entertainer.

Although the *One Thousand and One Nights* is a fictional account of Caliph Harun al-Rashid's supposed adventures, it does bear a striking resemblance to the real Caliph because he never failed to appreciate and admire the lighter and humorous side of life. As an intelligent and cultured man, he enjoyed life to its fullest and did so without making a mockery of his faith and beliefs in any way.

Though Caliph Harun transformed Baghdad into one of the world's most advanced and dazzling cities, he did not like its intense heat and hot climate. Throughout his reign, he went back and forth from one city to another in search of his ideal location and environment. He preferred a cool, lively and refreshing breeze which, of course, was obvious by its absence in Baghdad. After a long quest for his ideal location, he finally settled in the ancient Roman city of Callinicum. It had been transformed by his grandfather al-Mansur into a thriving metropolis. Later renamed al-Rafiqa, it is today located in Syria. In 802 CE, Harun went to perform yet another *hajj* and this time he took his sons Muhammad (Caliph al-Amin) and Abdullah (Caliph al-Ma'mun) with him. They visited the cities of Makkah and Madinah, where he distributed huge sums of money to the locals and also introduced his sons, and future successors, to the people of Makkah and Madinah; the Caliph was only thirty-six at the time.

On his return from *hajj*, he sensed something was not right in his court and his response took everyone around him by complete surprise. He removed the Barmakids, namely the vizier Yahya and his two sons Ja'far and Fadl, from their high-ranking government posts and placed them under house arrest. Ja'far was eventually murdered. Harun's drastic and heavy-handed action against his keen supporters continues to baffle historians to this day. As expected, without the support and guidance of his loyal and somewhat flamboyant Barmakid viziers, he struggled to maintain peace and stability throughout the Abbasid Empire. This prompted him to appoint al-Fadl ibn Rabi, the son of the great vizier Rabi, who had served his grandfather al-Mansur and his father al-Mahdi very loyally, to the post of Chief Minister. However, al-Fadl ibn Rabi also struggled to maintain the peace and security of the Abbasid Empire.

During the final years of his reign, Harun became occupied with military campaigns against the Byzantines and his political opponents at home. He died of illness at the age of forty-three, during a military expedition to Persia. He was buried in the ancient city of Tus. Before his death, he stipulated that his son al-Amin should succeed him as Caliph and he, in turn, was to be succeeded by al-Ma'mun. By this, he hoped to avoid a lengthy succession battle after his death, but his plans did not work out as he hoped.

All in all, with the death of Caliph Harun al-Rashid, a glorious chapter in Islamic history came to an abrupt end. As one of the Muslim world's most influential rulers, he is today famous both in the East and the West for his wide-ranging contributions to the rise and development of Islamic culture and civilisation.

29

Zubaidah bint Ja'far
(b.766 - d.831 CE) / (b.149 - d.216 AH)

There were many Abbasid princesses. However, one of the best-known was Zubaidah. Her birthdate remains unknown although it is known that she was a year younger than her husband Harun. Interestingly, she is famously known as Zubaidah, which is a pet name, given to her out of love by her grandfather, Caliph al-Mansur, because she was exceedingly beautiful with softness and white skin. The name means 'the best of something' or the 'cream of the best'. Her actual name at birth was Sukhainah or Amat al-Aziz. After she gave birth to Ja'far, she acquired the *kunya* (honourable name) of Umm Ja'far (Mother of Ja'far). She was married to Harun al-Rashid (chapter 28), who was the fifth Abbasid caliph who ruled for twenty-three years. Zubaidah was his sweetheart queen. She was related to many caliphs and lived during their times of rule.

Zubaidah loved the Qur'an. She had learnt the Qur'an, *Hadith* and Arabic literature enthusiastically. She was equally interested in science and literature, so much so that she allocated grants inviting poets, scientists and literary figures to Baghdad. Her devotion and love for the Qur'an and passion for listening to its recitation was such that she engaged a hundred women who recited the Qur'an day and night. It is recorded that the constant recitation of the Qur'an in the palace sounded like a beehive and wherever in the palace she went she could hear the verses echo. Moreover, her life was a model of a very devout and religious Muslimah who never missed a *salat*. Zubaidah was also constant with her *saum*. She had performed *hajj* many times, often making the 900-mile trip from Baghdad to Makkah. She once travelled for *hajj* on foot.

At the same time, her lifestyle was rather imperial and majestic. Her luxury was unmatched in the boundaries and environment of royalties. Zubaidah would spend thousands of *dinars* on a single dress. It is said that her footwear was studded with diamonds and pearls. To create an aromatic atmosphere, her palaces were lighted with candles of amber. It has also been noted that Zubaida was a trendsetter for the style of ladies of the ruling family and women of Baghdad. They were keen to follow her fashionable designs. Zubaidah loved natural silk and preferred brilliant colours. In addition to all this, her expenses for her kitchen exceeded more than ten thousand *dirhams* every day. Many hundreds of people lived and relied on her kitchen.

Her grandfather Caliph Mansur made special arrangements for her education. Over time, she developed a charming and eloquent speech. As a result, Zubaidah gained a highly influential position as his first lady. It was known that her husband arranged advisory sessions with her many times and for many reasons. People also knew that she always made appropriate and wise decisions. The books of history record that she controlled all the authorities during the absence of her husband when he was engaged in wars. As a result, she is credited with many outstanding achievements that still are named after her.

Zubaidah was deeply concerned about public welfare. She wanted to improve communal services and other civic structures through charitable works. To achieve these, she happily and generously spent on them. The road that connected Kufa, Baghdad and Makkah during the Abbasid period is known as the Darb Zubaidah (Zubaidah's trail) after Zubaiydah. She constructed travel inns and lodges on this route. It is said that one of the roads would be buried under severe sandstorms. As the area was a vast desert, it meant that travellers strayed and could not find the road. Zubaidah invested a vast amount of money to build a wall along both sides of the road to prevent the sandstorms from covering them. This 900-mile-long Darb Zubaidah also became a means for rich and powerful people to compete in charitable projects. Some of these projects were named after their sponsors, and so there was competition among rich donors. Along the road, wells, pools, mosques, stations, forts, houses and police posts were erected to provide welfare and safety to the pilgrims and their animals. There were tall minarets to identify the places and at night; these towers were lit with fire to guide the caravans in the right direction. These structures were well-built and survived for many centuries thereafter. Economically and culturally, this long trail helped pilgrims to tell stories about their own countries;, scholars taught and delivered sermons and businesses flourished.

However, Zubaidah's outstanding and long-lasting monumental humanitarian service was the construction of a canal. It was to become a landmark in the history of hydro-engineering. Before Harun al-Rashid became the Caliph, there had been serious water shortages in Makkah. During one of her *hajj*, Zubaidah experienced a drought and saw for herself the awful impact of it on the pilgrims and locals. As a person with concern for the welfare of people, she was deeply saddened and moved, like everyone else. Water became expensive and people and animals were in danger, but she was determined to solve the problem instantly.

As a queen, she gathered the best engineers and architects from different areas and instructed them to explore springs in the mountainous region of Makkah. It was a massive task, if not impossible to build a canal because of the rocky surfaces. After surveying for months, two springs were found. One was along the route to the famous city of Taif, which was about twenty-five kilometres away. To bring water from there to Makkah was not easy at all. Zubaidah was warned that the cost would be extremely high. As she was determined, generous and ambitious, she authorised the project. The constructors started it straight away and after three long years, the canal was ready. The cost is said to have exceeded millions of *dinars*.

One day, Zubaidah was relaxing in her palace along the bank of the River Tigris and was presented with the bill. She ignored the documents as she did not want to know about the bill. She announced that she had left all the paperwork to be settled on the Day of Judgement because she had initiated the canal to please Allah. She also declared she would pay those whom she owes any amount and if anyone owned her anything, then she forgave them. After some time, the canal ran up to Arafat and Mina. The canal served pilgrims and locals for over a thousand years. It was known as Ayn Zubaidah and its remains can still be seen today.

Zubaidah was also incredibly fond of learning and honoured the scholars. She sponsored a group of *Ulama* (scholars) to promote and spread Islamic learning. She was living at the time of Imam Abu Yusuf, the famous *Hanafi* scholar, with whom she had intellectual conversation. Zubaidah's courage, wisdom and piety inspired respect and appreciation among the public. She excelled in many subjects. She wrote poetry, excelled in Arabic literature and was a patroness of the arts. She was intelligent, a sound thinker and literary-minded. Some people have compared her education with those of the famous scholars of her time.

Zubaidah had a son named Muhammad Al-Amin. He was six months younger than his half-brother, Ali Al-Mamun whose mother was a Marajel. Zubaidah appealed to her husband, Caliph Harun, to nominate her son Amin as the next crown prince. However, Caliph Harun selected Al-Amin as his immediate successor but also nameds al-Mamun as his heir. Harun did this to maintain unity but this arrangement later failed. Harun also positioned al-Qasim as the third successor. By making this arrangement, Harun annoyed his wife. As expected, al-Amin did not live up to the expected standards from the start. His conflict with his brother intensified and, in the end, al-Amin was killed. Zubaiydah was a very graceful but astute lady. She overcame her grief and then wrote to al-Mamun saying that 'I congratulate the new caliph on his appointment. I have lost a son (al-Amin), but he was replaced by another of my sons (al-Mamun) that I did not give birth to'. These words touched al-Mamun because he was also raised by Zubaidah when his mother died soon after his birth. So, al-Mamun rushed to her and swore that he was innocent of the death of his half-brother, al-Amin. Thereafter, Caliph al-Mamun gave her full respect and consulted her on important matters.

Zubaidah died many years after her husband. Both are famous characters in the One Thousand and One Night Tales. She was very dear to him and was a high-minded empress who took his responsibilities in his absence. She lived her life based on her faith and values. These inspired her to embody high morals and charateristics which shined in her words and deeds. Zubaidah supported scholars, poets and artists which contributed to the growth of knowledge and culture. She used her wealth in charitable works, especially along the pilgrimage route and for social development. She is one of the most renowned female figures in Islamic history due to her notable lineage and love for luxury and magnificent palaces. With these, her canal and religious devotion keep her legacy alive.

30

Al-Shafi'i
(b.767 - d.820 CE) / (b.150 - d.205 AH)

If Sharia (Islamic law) is a vast and complex subject, then the science of *usul al-fiqh* (Islamic jurisprudence) is even more complex and sophisticated. The Qur'an and *Sunnah* are two of the most important sources of *fiqh* (Islamic jurisprudence). But how these two sources should be analysed, interpreted and implemented in a constantly changing and expanding Islamic society soon occupied the minds of the early *ulama* (Islamic scholars) and *fuqaha* (jurists). Following the death of the Prophet, the Islamic State continued to expand rapidly, and new challenges began to confront the early Muslim community.

This prompted scores of leading Islamic scholars to carry out a systematic study of the Qur'an and the Prophetic *Sunnah*. They developed *usul al-fiqh* (the science of Islamic jurisprudence) to meet the challenges of their time. It is true that Abu Hanifah and his talented students like Zufar, Abu Yusuf and Muhammad pioneered the Islamic legal method, but after his death, Imam Abu Hanifah's students focused their attention more on the substantive parts of Islamic law, rather than continuing to refine the main principles and method of *usul al-fiqh*. This important and challenging task was undertaken by Imam al-Shafi'i. Today he is widely considered to be the 'father of the science of Islamic jurisprudence'.

Muhammad ibn Idris al-Shafi'i was born in the city of Gaza in southern Palestine. His family claimed to be direct descendants of the Prophet Muhammad. He grew up there and received elementary education in Arabic language and grammar. He committed the entire Qur'an to memory before he was seven. When Imam al-Shafi'i was still young, his father died, and this prompted his mother to migrate to their ancestral home in Makkah as her family members and close relatives of Yemeni origin lived at the time. He then received further training in Arabic grammar and literature and became skilled at archery. Here al-Shafi'i and his mother were forced to endure considerable personal and financial hardship. But, despite their miserable economic situation, his devout mother was keen to give her son a good start in life by continuing with his education.

From the outset, al-Shafi's exceptional memory and sharp intellect made him very dear to his teachers. According to his biographers, he could commit large collections of *Hadith* to memory with ease. Imam Malik's book of *Hadith al-Muwatta* (The Beaten Path) was a popular religious text at the time. All the brightest students of Islamic sciences were expected to learn it by heart. He consequently memorised this compilation of Prophetic traditions fully before he was fifteen years old. He mastered this book so well that he became an expert on the religious thought of Imam Malik. Al-Shafi'i then studied fiqh under the guidance of other great teachers who were respected jurists of their time.

Furthermore, the governor of Makkah was very impressed with al-Shafi'is intellectual abilities. So, he wrote a letter to the governor in Madinah to request that Imam Malik should teach al-Shafi'i, who was only twenty at the time. In Madinah, he devoted all his time and energy to learning *Hadith* and *fiqh*. He studied the *al-Muwatta* under Malik's personal supervision. Some of Malik's famous students at the time included scholars like Imam Muhammad ibn al-Hasan al-Shaybani, who came all the way from Iraq to attend Malik's lectures. Although he was happy to be in the company of such an illustrious group of Islamic legal minds, on a more personal level, he began to experience considerable financial hardship at the time.

Unlike the other students, he had no one to support him financially. However, because of his intellectual brilliance, Malik offered him a regular allowance which enabled him to complete his advanced education. His stay in Madinah proved very productive, so much so that Imam Malik later asked him to become his teaching assistant. By the time Malik died, Imam al-Shafi'i had already become recognised throughout Madinah as an outstanding Islamic scholar and jurist.

Deeply saddened by Malik's death, he soon left Madinah and returned to his native Makkah. Here, his reputation spread across the Hijaz on account of his vast knowledge of Islamic sciences. On one occasion, when the governor of Yemen happened to be in Makkah, he was informed about al-Shafi'is intellectual abilities and legal expertise. This prompted the governor to approach him and invite him to accompany him to Yemen. The governor promised to make him the Chief Justice of the city of Najran. The tall, slim and always perfectly dressed al-Shafi'i accepted the offer and moved to Yemen at the age of thirty-one.

However, his transition from the world of learning and teaching to the murky and uncertain world of politics and diplomacy did not go according to plan. As a gifted jurist and Islamic scholar, he was thoroughly clean, honest and trustworthy. He was also determined to uphold the truth and administer justice as fairly and equitably as he could. However, his strict and uncompromising application of Islamic law did not go down too well with certain groups in the corridors of power in Najran. Unaware of the unease and dissatisfaction he was creating within the local governmental circles, al-Shafi'i continued to apply Islamic law without any fear or favouritism. This eventually brought him into direct conflict with members of the ruling political and religious elites. They were keen to have him dismissed so they falsely accused al-Shafi'i of sympathising with a rebellious Shi'a faction which was bitterly opposed to the Abbasid rulers at the time.

The charge of treason levelled against al-Shafi'i was both false and unproven, but he was still found guilty of protecting the rebellious Shi'as. He was chained from head to toe by the authorities in Najran and deported to the highest Abbasid court in Baghdad. The thirty-six-year-old Imam al-Shafi'i was summoned by Harun al-Rashid, the famous Abbasid Caliph, to appear before him. He also summoned the other alleged conspirators to answer the charges. The following day, the Imam went to the Caliph's court and, one by one, he refuted all the charges levelled against him. Harun al-Rashid was so impressed with his vast knowledge and logical arguments that he engaged him in debate and discussion for a long period. They discussed the finer points of Islamic theology, jurisprudence, logic and Greek thoughts. As a great patron of learning and scholarship, the Caliph deeply admired al-Shafi'i's brilliant mind.

By coincidence, Imam Muhammad al-Shaybani (Shafi'i's old classmate in Madinah), happened to be the Chief Justice of Baghdad at the time. So, he supported Imam al-Shafi'i and requested the Caliph to free al-Shafi'i. He said that al-Shafi'i was one of the most famous scholars of his generation. The Caliph not only spared Shafi'i's life, but he also requested that he should stay in Baghdad and help him promote learning and scholarship throughout the land.

The Imam was relieved to have been spared. He settled in Baghdad and vowed never to become a government official again. Instead, he resumed his career as an academic and researcher in Islamic sciences, for that was his real passion. In Baghdad, he conducted advanced research in *fiqh* and *Hadith* under the guidance of its leading scholars. He regularly attended the lectures of Imam Muhammad al-Shaybani, who was one of the leading students of Imam Abu Hanifah. Imam al-Shaybani was considered to be one of the great scholars of Islam. He was an outstanding authority on Islamic law at the time. Imam al-Shafi'i learned *hanafi* jurisprudence under al-Shaybani's guidance and became an expert in the legal thought of this school.

During his heated discussions with the leading *hanafi* scholars, Imam al-Shafi'i deliberately emphasised the significance of *Hadith* in the development of Islamic legal principles and practices. He felt *qiyas* (analogical deduction) played a far greater role within the *hanafi* legal method than was necessary. He highlighted the importance of relying on Prophetic *Hadith* where it was possible to do so. Not surprisingly, he emerged from his discussions with the *hanafis* as a great champion of Prophetic *Hadith*. That is not to say, however, that the *hanafi* scholars did not uphold the *Hadith*. On the contrary, the hanafis intensely obeyed authentic *Hadith* but, unlike the *malikis* and Imam Shafi'i himself, they placed greater emphasis on the need for human individuality.

Nevertheless, it is also very true that *hanafi* legal thought is characterised by its considerable reliance on the construction of principles from the Qur'an and the authentic *sunnah* of the Prophet. Imam Shafi'i was acutely aware of this. So, he deliberately engaged the *hanafis* in discussion on the finer points of their legal thought. By doing this, he successfully mastered the legal thought of both Imam Abu Hanifah and Imam Malik. This was a remarkable achievement for al-Shafi'i. He was now able to analyse, refine and even critique the legal thought of two of the Muslim world's most influential jurists.

Imam al-Shafi'i rightly considered Imam Abu Hanifah to be the father of Islamic legal thought. He considered Imam Malik to be a great authority on *Hadith*. But he also knew that the science of Islamic jurisprudence had to be systematically developed and codified for the benefit of future generations. Of course, he knew this was not an easy task. He was more than qualified to undertake this challenging but important work. His success in this earned him a unique place in the intellectual history of Islam, as he was the first to systematically develop the science of Islamic jurisprudence.

In 804 CE, Imam al-Shafi'i left Baghdad and moved to Syria, and from there he went to Makkah where he began to deliver regular lectures on *fiqh* and *Hadith* at the *Haram al-Sharif* (the Sacred Mosque). Hundreds of students, including the famous Imam Ahmad ibn Hanbal (see chapter 31), travelled from across the Muslim world to attend his inspiring talks on all aspects of Islam. After six years of teaching and travelling across Syria and Arabia, al-Shafi'i returned to Baghdad to find al-Ma'mun (see chapter 33), the son and successor of Caliph Harun al-Rashid, on the Abbasid throne.

Al-Ma'mun immediately asked Imam al-Shafi'i to become the Chief Justice of Baghdad. But, because of his previous bad experience in Najran, he politely turned down the offer. Moreover, since al-Ma'mun was a champion of the heretical Mu'tazilite creed, al-Shafi'i — like the other traditionalist scholars of the time — considered him to be a mischief-maker. Al-Ma'mun did not like al-Shafi'i's rejection. The Imam realised the gravity of the situation and quietly left Baghdad and proceeded to Egypt.

At the time, Egypt was a very peaceful and intellectually favourable place. Here he met many famous Islamic scholars and jurists. He frequently engaged in discussion and debate with these scholars on different matters of *fiqh* and *Hadith*. This helped him to further polish his own ideas on these subjects. Once he was convinced that he had fully grasped the complexities of Islamic law, he sat down to create a systematic and coherent theory of Islamic legal thought. He took into consideration the views of the *Hanafis* as well as the *Malikis*. By doing this, he presented a comprehensive and equally refreshing explanation of Islamic legal principles to address the new challenges of his time.

He recorded his thoughts in his celebrated *Kitab al-Umm* (The Book of Essence) and *al-Risalah* (The Treatise). In these two books, he — for the very first time in Islamic history — systematically formulated the fundamental principles of the science of Islamic jurisprudence. He studied under the guidance of both the *Hanafi* and *Maliki* scholars and developed his own method of the scriptural sources of Islam. In the process, he became the pioneer of *usul al-fiqh*.

The balanced approach adopted by Imam Shafi'i regarding the revealed sources of Islam enabled him to emphasise the importance of *Hadith* while he was in the company of the *Hanafis*. He was also able to highlight the role of human nature and its frailties when he was with the *Malikis*. In short, by harmonising the legal methods of Imam Abu Hanifa and Imam Malik, Imam Shafi'i created a new, comprehensive and original legal synthesis. He was so successful in his task that a Shafi'i *madhhab* (or school of legal thought) emerged and spread across the Muslim world.

Today, this *madhhab* is widely followed in Egypt, Yemen, Southern India, Indonesia, Malaysia and parts of South America and East Africa. Imam al-Shafi'i was blessed with an extraordinary memory and remarkably sharp intellect. He left his permanent mark on the intellectual history of Islam as one of its greatest legal theorists. He died and was buried in al-Fustat, Egypt at the age of fifty-three. The Ayyubid ruler Afdal built an impressive mausoleum, which still stands to this day, as a tribute to his memory.

31

Ahmad ibn Hanbal
(b.778 - d.855 CE) / (b.163 - d.241 AH)

Islamic history is filled with scholars who distinguished themselves by the breadth of their learning and courage. These scholars were both pious and extremely knowledgeable in Islamic principles and practices. They cared little about the wealth and material possessions of this world. They humbled themselves before their Creator during the darkness of the night and continued their quest for knowledge and wisdom during the day. They also endured considerable personal and financial hardship. They were often made to suffer for their faith and principles, but they never bowed before a King or Queen. To them, the life of this world was like an illusion, without a reality of its own.

The search for truth, justice, equality and the welfare of the poor and needy became their main mission in life. They were men of remarkable character, enduring personality and deep courage and determination. Such exemplary scholars appeared at various times in Islamic history, and they fulfilled their service with patience, perseverance and great success. Imam Ahmad ibn Hanbal was one such powerful scholar and reformer who emerged to defend traditional Islamic beliefs at a critical time in Islamic history. He left his permanent mark and became known as one of the most successful scholars of Islam.

Ahmad ibn Muhammad ibn Hanbal was born into the noble Arab tribe of al-Shayban. Ahmad's grandfather, Hanbal, occupied a prominent position as governor of the province of Sarakhs under the Umayyads (Sarakhs is a city in Khorasan province, Iran). His father, Muhammad, was a valiant warrior who participated in a *jihad* (military expedition) led by the Umayyads and died on the battlefield. Ahmad was about two years old when his father died. He was brought up in very difficult economic circumstances by his devout mother, Safiya. He attended his local schools and successfully memorised the entire Qur'an before he was ten. Influenced by his mother, Ahmad began to study *Hadith* at the age of sixteen and fell deeply in love with the subject. He was not only a bright student but was also deeply religious during his early years. His reliable character and friendly personality were very dear to his teachers.

During this period, he worked as a clerk at his local post office to supplement his family's insufficient income. He regularly drafted letters for the illiterate villages free of charge. So he combined his education in *fiqh* (Islamic jurisprudence) and *Hadith* under the guidance of Imam Abu Yusuf with his extra-curricular activities. Abu Yusuf was one of the foremost students of Imam Abu Hanifah and an outstanding Islamic scholar and jurist in his own right. Although Abu Hanifah died about fourteen years before Ahmad was born, he was very fortunate to study *Hadith* and *fiqh* under Imam Abu Yusuf who was one of the most gifted jurists of his generation. Ahmad attended Imam Abu Yusuf's lectures regularly and became thoroughly familiar with *Hanafi fiqh*.

He then studied *Hadith* and *fiqh* for another four years under the guidance of Haitham, who was one of the top scholars of *Hadith* in Baghdad. As the political capital of the Muslim world and a thriving city, Baghdad attracted some of the Muslim world's most prominent scholars to live and teach there. Eager to complete his education, Ahmad then attended the classes of some great teachers. He rapidly learnt Islamic knowledge and wisdom. His devotion, dedication and commitment to his studies, especially of Prophetic *Hadith,* was such that he often left his home well before the dawn prayer (*fajr*) and waited for his teachers to arrive to begin the first class of the day. After completing his studies under the renowned scholars of Baghdad, he travelled to other major centres of Islamic learning such as Basrah Kufah, Makkah, Madinah, Yemen and Syria to study *Hadith*.

During his travels of many years, he met Imam al-Shafi'i (see chapter 30), who was living in Makkah at the time. Although Ahmad was much younger than al-Shafi'i, the latter was deeply impressed by his vast knowledge of Islam. Many years later, these two luminaries of Islam met again: this time in Baghdad. By then Imam al-Shafi'i had already developed his theories of Islamic jurisprudence rigorously and systematically. Likewise, Imam Ahmad became widely recognised as an outstanding scholar of *Hadith*. He had mastered all the complexities and details of this subject under the guidance of the Yemeni scholar, Imam Ibn Hammam, the author of the Musannaf. Here in Baghdad, the two men regularly engaged in discussion on the finer points of fiqh and *Hadith*. Imam al-Shafi'i soon acknowledged Imam Ahmad's superiority in *Hadith* and regularly consulted him on difficult issues relating to *Hadith*.

Since Ahmad's main passion in life was the pursuit of knowledge, he happily travelled long distances in search of Islamic knowledge and wisdom. He was not one of those who expected his teachers to come to him. He went out of his way to visit his teachers to learn from them. There is a story about this. He first met his tutor Abd al-Razzaq ibn Hammam in Makkah during the *hajj*. His colleague Yahya, the teacher of Imam al-Bukhari, suggested that they should start learning from him there and then. However, Ahmad disagreed with him and instead, he travelled all the way to San'a, the capital of Yemen, to study *Hadith* under Abd al-Razzaq. As an honest and passionate seeker of knowledge, he was happy to spend his money and tolerate hardship in his search for knowledge. But he never liked to compromise his beliefs and principles in the process. Ahmad's collaboration with al-Shafi'i proved extremely beneficial for him for several reasons. Before this, he had been busy writing and memorising *Hadith* and fiqh, but Imam al-Shafi'i helped him to develop a critical approach to these subjects.

As an outstanding analyst, Imam al-Shafi'i explained to him his theories of Islamic jurisprudence, including all the complexities involved in constructing and deduction deducting the principles of *usul al-fiqh* (science of Islamic jurisprudence). This enabled Ahmad to revisit the large quantity of *Hadith* he had learned. His critical examination of *Hadith* literature enabled him to establish their relevance to Islamic law and legal theory. This represented a major turning point in Imam Ahmad's intellectual journey. He was now in a position to develop his own approach to *fiqh* (jurisprudence), thanks to his colossal knowledge of *Hadith*, the sayings of the *Sahabah* and the *tabiun* (successors of the companions). Ahmad's mastery of both *Hadith* and *fiqh* was then publicly acknowledged by Imam al-Shafi'i himself when he said: 'I am leaving Baghdad when there is none more pious, nor a greater jurist than Ahmad ibn Hanbal.' He was about forty at the time.

Normally, a scholar of Ahmad's standard and accomplishment would have started his own religious seminary long before he reached forty, but he did not do so. Why wait so long? Some historians say that he followed the Prophet's example. That is to say, since the Prophet did not attain his Prophethood and began to propagate Islam until he was forty, Imam Ahmad waited till he reached his fortieth birthday. Others say he decided not to teach while his own teachers were still alive, out of respect for them. Interestingly Imam al-Shafi'i died in the year Ahmad turned forty. It is not clear whether his death played a part in his decision to start teaching. Perhaps it was a combination of all these factors which encouraged him to set up his own class.

Either way, Ahmad started teaching *Hadith* and *fiqh* at the age of forty. He soon gathered around him a large following of devout believers. Having suffered considerable financial hardship during his student days, he gave preference to the financially poor students, especially those who were not in a position to pay for tuition. When he delivered lectures on *Hadith* and fiqh, his students listened to him in absolute silence and respect. Often the local public came along to hear him explain *Hadith* and *fiqh* in his unique style. It was not long before his reputation spread in and around Baghdad. According to some historians, his lectures were attended by hundreds of students at a time. He was not overwhelmed by the mass attention he now received. Imam Ahmad continued to lead a simple and austere lifestyle, far removed from the wealth and luxuries of this world.

If any of his well-wishers sent him any money or gifts, he gave them away to the poor and needy. On several occasions, the Caliph sent him parcels of gifts, but he refused to accept them. When his sons asked him why he refused to accept such gifts, he explained that giving and taking gifts was not unlawful. It was perfectly acceptable — and even encouraged — to give and accept gifts. He also stated that one could even perform *hajj* with money given as a gift. However, he refused to accept the Caliph's gifts due to caution and personal abstinence. Like so many other great Islamic scholars (such as al-Shafi'i and al-Bukhari), he refused to accept money or gifts from the rulers of his time just in case they happened to come from an unlawful source.

Instead, he lived on income from a small, rented apartment he owned. When he ran out of money, which he did regularly, he used to skip meals. On one occasion he became so desperate that he could not afford to replace his old and worn-out clothes. So, when the locals offered to buy him new ones, he politely refused. Since his poverty was self-imposed, Ahmad maintained his self-respect and dignity by not accepting anything without paying for it. Only when his situation became very desperate, did he accept small amounts of money, but always on the condition that he repaid it later. His sincerity, simplicity and deep insight into Islamic teachings made him very popular with the public in Baghdad.

He lived at a time when Mu'tazilism (philosophical rationalism) became the main belief of the Abbasid Empire under the stewardship of Caliph al-Ma'mun (see chapter 33). As a champion of rationalism, the Caliph and his immediate successors (Caliphs Mu'tasim Bi'llah and al-Wathiq Bi'llah) turned Mu'tazilism into an official creed of the State and they also imposed it on the people by force. After a Caliphal order was issued which demanded that all the scholars in Baghdad had to follow the Mu'tazilite creed and anyone who refused to do so would be severely punished, Ahmad's life was suddenly turned upside down. The Mu'tazilites believed that the Qur'an was created. This was contrary to the traditional Islamic view, which stated that the Qur'an was the uncreated Word of Allah. Many traditional Islamic scholars flatly refused to accept the Caliphal order.

However, when these scholars were threatened with severe punishment by the ruling Abbasid elites, most of them pretended to follow the Mu'tazilite creed to save their skins. Only a handful of scholars continued to reject the Caliph's decree. Ahmad was one of them. The Caliph then ordered all the scholars who rejected his order to be brought to his palace in chains, they all surrendered except one. That fearless scholar was Ahmad ibn Hanbal.

He was brought before Caliph Mu'tasim Bi'llah chained from head to toe. The Caliph questioned him about his beliefs for more than four days and urged him to change his views. Ahmad remained firm and refused. The battle between Islamic traditionalism and philosophical rationalism was now full-blown and raging. When it became clear that Ahmad would not give up, his persecutors threatened him with severe chastisement, but he remained defiant. Ahmad was then beaten until the whip broke into two pieces. He was then dragged before the Caliph for more questioning, but again, he refused to budge an inch. The Caliph then ordered more punishment. This time he was tortured so severely that eyewitnesses said even an elephant would not have been able to endure such treatment. Yet Ahmad remained as firm as ever. He refused to bow before the menace of rationalism, which at the time was threatening to undermine the very foundation of Islam. His courage and bravery in the face of such barbarism even won over his opponents.

As expected, soon his name and fame spread across the Islamic world like wildfire. His peers poured much praise on him for keeping the flame of Islamic traditionalism alive. One renowned scholar of the time remarked, 'When you find someone being affectionate on Ahmad ibn Hanbal, then know that he is a follower of the Prophet's tradition.' Imam Ahmad continued his struggle against the Mu'tazilites until Mutawakkil 'ala Allah became the next Abbasid ruler and reversed his predecessor's harsh policies. The new Caliph also freed Ahmad from captivity so that he could resume his normal activities. During this period, he wrote numerous books on *Hadith* and *fiqh* including his famous al-Musnad, which contains more than thirty thousand a *Hadith* and a large selection of views and opinions of the Prophet's companions about different aspects of Islam.

Imam Ahmad ibn Hanbal died and was buried in Baghdad at the age of around seventy-seven. After his death, a new school of Islamic legal thought emerged named after him. The *hanbali madhhab* is today followed mainly in Palestine and Saudi Arabia. His religious ideas and thoughts have influenced generations of influential Islamic scholars and reformers.

32

Al-Khwarizmi
(b.780 - d.847 CE)

The origin of all the physical sciences can be traced back in one way or another to mathematics. That is why mathematics is generally considered to be the mother of all these subjects. In its early days, mathematics showed itself in three different forms. These were arithmetic (counting with numbers), geometry (measurement of areas) and algebra (calculating using symbols and their relationships). These mathematical techniques enabled ancient people to think,; reason and express themselves in a precise way in their daily affairs. Although arithmetic is the first, and perhaps the most ancient, form of mathematics, very little is known about its origin. According to historians, archaeological excavations carried out in the Nile Valley and Mesopotamia have shown that counting was familiar to both ancient Egyptians and the Babylonians. The Chinese and Indians also developed their distinctive ways of counting, just as the Arabs used the position of their fingers to help them count during the time of the Prophet Muhammad.

Like the Greeks and the Romans before them, the Arabs also used their alphabet for counting purposes until the advent of Arabic numerals. Though the zero-based number system was known to the ancient Indians, it was the Muslims who invented the word 'zero'. It is derived from the Arabic *sifr*, meaning 'nothing' or 'nil'.

The Muslim mathematicians developed a rigorous decimal system which subsequently became known as the Arabic numerals. When the Muslim mathematicians were busy conducting complex and sophisticated mathematical equations in their research laboratories in Baghdad, Damascus, Cairo and Merv, the Europeans were struggling to perform simple mathematical calculations using Roman numerals. Trying to conduct a simple mathematical equation using Roman numerals was an uphill job; frankly, it was a hopeless task.

By contrast, the introduction of Arabic numerals represented nothing short of a major revolution in mathematical study. It helped the early Muslim mathematicians to develop and refine the entire subject of mathematics for the benefit of humanity. No other mathematician played a more pivotal role in the development of algebra and Arabic numerals than al-Khwarizmi. That is why he is today considered to be one of the greatest mathematical geniuses of all time.

Muhammad ibn Musa al-Khwarizmi was born in Khwarazm, in the Central Asian province of Khurasan. Khurasan at the time was a thriving centre of commerce and literary activities. Under the support of its ruling elites, schools and colleges mushroomed across the province. They taught both religious and scientific subjects and were studied by leading Muslim scholars and thinkers of the day. Al-Khwarizmi was born into a family where the search for knowledge was valued more than anything else. His family migrated to the district of Qurtrubulli, located on the outskirts of Baghdad when he was still a child.

Though very little is known about al-Khwarizmi's early life, it was the custom of the day for young children to attend their local schools and receive basic instruction in Arabic and traditional Islamic sciences. This was followed by more intensive training in Arabic grammar, literature, poetry, Islamic theology and philosophy. The students who were considered to be most capable and gifted by their tutors were then encouraged to pursue research in medicine, astronomy, alchemy and mathematics. This would widen their intellectual horizons. As an unusually talented student, al-Khwarizmi followed the standard curriculum of the day and soon impressed everyone with his mastery of the religious, philosophical and scientific knowledge of the time.

When al-Khwarizmi's reputation as a talented religious scholar, scientist and mathematician reached the corridors of power in Baghdad, the reigning Abbasid Caliph, Abdullah al-Ma'mun, invited him to join his celebrated *Bait al-Hikmah* (The House of Wisdom) in Baghdad. He was around forty at the time. Like his illustrious father, al-Ma'mun became a generous patron and supporter of philosophical and scientific research. In fact, he promoted learning, research and inquiry into all branches of learning and education. The *bait al-hikmah* was originally founded by Harun during his reign as Caliph (see chapter 28). It then became one of the Muslim world's most famous and influential libraries and centres of research under Caliph al-Ma'mun's patronage. He recruited some of the most talented philosophers, scientists, geographers and mathematicians of his time to this centre to teach and research in science, mathematics and philosophy.

As expected, al-Khwarizmi occupied a prominent position in *bait al-hikmah*. Here, he researched astronomy, geography, history, music and mathematics, which was his most favourite subject. The Caliph was deeply impressed by al-Khwarizmi's mathematical abilities and personally asked him to head the department of astronomical research at *Bait al-Hikmah*. He not only excelled in astronomy, but he also made groundbreaking contributions to a number of other scientific subjects. He authored an influential book on history entitled *Kitab al-Tarikh* (The Book of History). This book inspired other celebrated Muslim historians like al-Mas'udi (see chapter 44) and al-Tabari (see chapter 38) to produce their own works on the subject.

It was under Caliph Harun al-Rashid's sponsorship that pioneering Muslim scholars and translators first began to translate the scientific contributions of the ancient Greeks into Arabic. The Muslim scientists and mathematicians not only preserved ancient Greek intellectual heritage, but they also analysed the intellectual and cultural contributions of other ancient civilisations, including those of Persia, India and China. Their thirst for knowledge and wisdom inspired them to learn, embrace and refine the works of the ancients and make their original contributions to all the branches of knowledge.

According to some historians, al-Khwarizmi's quest for knowledge took him all the way to India, where he mastered traditional

Indian science and mathematics. It was also during his stay in India that he became familiar with the zero-based decimal system for the first time. Although it is not clear how long he stayed in India, he lived there for long enough to have gained proficiency in Sanskrit, as he was thoroughly familiar with this language. During this period, al-Khwarizmi discovered that the ancient Indians used a blank space to represent 'nothing' or 'nil' (*sunya*), which inspired him to coin the Arabic word *sifr* meaning 'nothing', just as its Latin equivalent, *ciphrium*, later came to denote 'zero'.

However, according to other historians, there is no credible evidence to suggest that al-Khwarizmi visited India. On the contrary, they argue that he became familiar with Indian arithmetic and astronomy from translated manuscripts which were available in Baghdad at the time. Either way, his discovery of the concept of 'zero' enabled him to lay the foundations of a new decimal system. This system is today widely known as Arabic numerals, and in so doing he changed the study of mathematics forever.

By all accounts, al-Khwarizmi's contribution to mathematics was both unique and unprecedented. The originality of his mathematical contribution is most evident from the fact that the word 'algebra' was derived directly from the title of his famous book on the subject, entitled *Kitab al-Mukhtasar fi Hisab al-Jabr wa'l Muqabalah* (The Summarised Treatise on Calculation by Completion and Balancing).

This book was one of the first of its kind written by a Muslim. In this book, he systematically defined and developed algebra for the first time in the history of mathematics. Later, it was translated into Latin by Robert of Chester in 1145 CE. This groundbreaking mathematical treatise was divided into five chapters. The author systematically examined different dimensions of algebra in each chapter.

In the first chapter, al-Khwarizmi discussed the nature of linear and quadratic equations. He showed how they could be explained and resolved without providing any demonstrative proof. He also divided quadratic equations into six categories to highlight their separate geometrical configurations. During his investigations, he discovered that quadratic equations had two different roots. One being positive which he accepted, and the other being negative which he rejected. In so doing, he developed a fresh approach to the study and exploration of such equations.

In the next chapter, al-Khwarizmi showed how quadratic equations could be resolved in a demonstrative way by using geometric methods. In the third and fourth chapters, he explored the problems posed by multiplication and explained how differences between sums, squares and methods of locating square roots of hidden or unknown quantities in equations could be resolved. In the fifth and final chapter of the book, he developed solutions for many mathematical problems using different algebraic formulae. As expected, these mathematical problems were complex and multi-layered, and they required original and imaginative solutions, but al-Khwarizmi was able to define and resolve them, one by one, in a masterly fashion. Indeed, he used around eight hundred different demonstrative equations to show how calculations of integration and equation could be performed.

Al-Khwarizmi's work in arithmetic and algebra was of very high standard. It would not be an exaggeration to say that he was the pioneer, or father, of these important branches of mathematics. His book on arithmetic entitled 'The Book of Aggregation and Division in Indian Mathematics' was not only a pioneering mathematical contribution, but it also became a hugely influential book. After Bon Compagni translated it into Latin in 1157 CE, it became a popular textbook on arithmetic throughout medieval Europe.

A copy of this translation is still available to this day in Rome. The book also introduced Arabic numerals and the concept of 'zero' or 'cipher' into the Western world for the very first time. By doing this, it helped to popularise the application of basic arithmetic in every area of modern life. Al-Khwarizmi's scholarship had such an extensive influence on Western science and technology that he became known as 'Algorithm' across Europe, and throughout the centuries, his Latinised name became synonymous with the word 'arithmetic' in the West.

Today 'algorithm' refers to a technique which is used in the field of computer science for carrying out analysis using recurring methods. Without al-Khwarizimi's seminal contributions in arithmetic, algebra, trigonometry and other branches of mathematics, it would not have been possible for Nicolaus Copernicus, Johannes Kepler, Galileo Galilei, Sir Isaac Newton and others to achieve as much as they did in the field of astronomy, physics, mathematics and chemistry. Thanks also to al-Khwarizmi, today people can travel to space, fly aeroplanes, watch satellite television and count to a zillion without any problems or difficulties. By revolutionising the study of mathematics, he completely revolutionised our vision of ourselves and, indeed, our vision of the future for the benefit of the whole of humanity.

If scientists like Sir Isaac Newton were a rare breed, then geniuses like al-Khwarizmi were even rarer. His contribution to mathematics aside, al-Khwarizmi was also a brilliant astronomer and geographer. Once, when Caliph al-Ma'mun commissioned him to measure the meridian from a location close to the Euphrates, he accomplished the task by inventing an astronomical device which was far superior to anything the Greeks had produced. In fact, he not only accurately measured and determined the sphericity of the earth, but he also suggested ways in which the process could be made easier in the future, by improving the device he had invented.

Towards the end of his life, he authored a book on geography entitled, 'The Book on the Shape of the Earth'. In this book, he corrected Ptolemy's misconceptions about different aspects of geography, geology and other related sciences. The publication of this book also marked the beginning of the science of geography in the Muslim world. All subsequent Muslim scientists and geographers were one way or another influenced by this pioneering book. In total, al-Khwarizmi authored more than a dozen books on all the sciences of his time. He died at the age of sixty-seven and was laid to rest in Baghdad.

33

Abdullah al-Ma'mun
(b.786 - d.833 CE) / (b.170 - d.218 AH)

The question of political succession has often been a major stumbling block in Islamic political history. In the absence of any clear religious guidelines, political succession was often decided through long political struggles or internal fighting between opposing claimants to the Caliphate. The celebrated Abbasid Caliph Harun al-Rashid was keen to avoid a similar conflict after his death. So he took the unusual step of appointing his successor during his lifetime. According to the agreement prepared by Harun, he was to be succeeded by his son, Muhammad, who became known as Caliph al-Amin (b. 787-d. 813 CE). It also stated that al-Amin was to be succeeded by his brother, Abdullah, who later became known as Caliph al-Ma'mun. Thus, as per Harun's instructions, Muhammad succeeded his illustrious father and ruled for four years during which he fought tooth and nail to prevent his brother Abdullah from becoming Caliph after him.

Instead, al-Amin nominated his son, Musa, as his heir and thus openly broke the oath of allegiance he had signed with his father. As expected, al-Ma'mun accused his brother of being a traitor. This set the two brothers against each other, leading to considerable political in-fighting and loss of life. The scene of devastation brought upon the house of Harun al-Rashid would have turned him in his grave. However, al-Amin's dishonourable actions earned him nothing but disgrace, while his brother, al-Ma'mun, not only went on to become one of the Muslim world's most major rulers but also carved out an important place for himself in the intellectual history of Islam.

Abdullah al-Ma'mun ibn Harun al-Rashid was born in Baghdad after his father succeeded to the Abbasid throne at a young age. Al-Mamun's mother came from an Arabian family. She was a beautiful lady who was deeply adored by her husband, Caliph Harun al-Rashid. Unfortunately, she died while al-Ma'mun was still in his infancy. The young boy was therefore brought up by his father. Being a wise and kind father, Harun showered his children with much wealth and luxury, whilst also ensuring that they received a thorough education. There was obvious tension and jealousy between Harun's family. This was between the supporters of his son al-Amin by his Arab wife Zubaida bint Ja'far (b. 766-d. 831 CE), who was an Abbasid princess, and the supporters of al-Ma'mun (whose mother came from a lower-class Arab family). But Harun treated all his children fairly without showing any favouritism.

Keen to educate his children in both the religious and scientific subjects of the day, the Caliph invited the leading scholars to come and teach al-Ma'mun. He thus received a thorough education in Arabic language, literature and aspects of Islamic sciences. Since Malik ibn Anas (see chapter 24) of Madinah was one of the most outstanding Islamic scholars of his generation, Harun sent a letter to the respected scholar requesting him to come to Baghdad to teach his children. Imam Malik turned down the offer, saying that true seekers of knowledge do not expect knowledge to come and knock on their doors; instead, they go out in search of knowledge. The Caliph understood exactly what the wise scholar meant and immediately set out for Madinah, with his children, to attend Malik's lectures. However, according to some historians, al-Amin and al-Ma'mun did not attend Malik's lectures. Either way, young al-Ma'mun acquired considerable knowledge of Islamic sciences and became thoroughly familiar with the Qur'an. The Caliph then placed him under the care of his Chief Minister, Ja'far al-Barmaki, who trained him in both political and civil administration.

Like his father, al-Ma'mun was a handsome young man who was blessed with a sharp intellect and polished diplomatic skills.

When al-Ma'mun was only twelve, Harun asked all members of his family to pledge their allegiance to al-Ma'mun as a future Caliph. The deed of political succession – prepared by Harun and preserved in its entirety by the historian al-Tabari – stipulated that al-Ma'mun would become Caliph after the death of his brother al-Amin, thus ensuring a smooth transition of power from one to the other. However, the hierarchy within Harun's armed forces preferred al-Amin over al-Ma'mun, but the Caliph was determined that al-Ma'mun should not in any way be disadvantaged or sidelined after his death. He, therefore, personally inscribed al-Ma'mun's name on the deed of succession and thus ensured that he was in line to ascend the Abbasid throne after al-Amin.

Al-Ma'mun became an able and experienced political and civil administrator, eventually being appointed governor of the large province of Khurasan. As expected, his successful reign as governor of Khurasan enhanced his political power and personal standing within the royal family. Thus, by the time his father fell out with Ja'far the Barmakid and sentenced him to death, al-Ma'mun was already recognised as an able and experienced provincial administrator.

Caliph Harun al-Rashid died at the age of forty-three. During his reign of twenty-two years, he completely transformed the fortunes of the Abbasid Empire. He restored peace, order and security throughout his vast empire. Baghdad, the capital of the Abbasid Empire, also became a sophisticated city, boasting hundreds of renowned schools, colleges, libraries, hospitals and markets. In other words, under Harun's sponsorship, Baghdad became one of the Muslim world's most famous educational, cultural and architectural centres. Unfortunately, his son and successor, Caliph al-Amin, failed to live up to his father's high standards. Although Harun had twelve sons, only al-Amin, al-Ma'mun and al-Mu'tasim were groomed for leadership by their father. All three of them occupied prominent political positions during their father's reign.

After Harun's death, the three brothers remained faithful to the deed of succession prepared by their father and regularly exchanged messages of peace, support and goodwill. This state of affairs continued until Caliph al-Amin, urged by his chief political advisor al-Fadl ibn Rabi, openly violated the deed of succession. Since al-Fadl hated al-Ma'mun and thought Caliph Harun had granted him too much power and autonomy, he convinced Caliph al-Amin to remove his name from the deed of succession, and instead nominate his son as his successor. This was not only an insensitive move; it also proved to be fatal for Caliph al-Amin who now found himself at odds with his brothers al-Ma'mun and Mu'tasim.

Al-Ma'mun was based at his headquarters at Merv (in present-day Turkmenistan), at the time the provincial capital of Khurasan. He was urged by his advisor al-Fadl ibn Sahl not to give up his claim to the Caliphate. In other words, beneath the surface, the two Fadls were in reality engaged in a bitter power struggle of their own. Each Fadl was determined to preserve their own personal interests, wealth and position. Al-Fadl ibn Rabi was an Arab so he supported Caliph al-Amin, who was the son of an Arab princess, and was determined to keep power in the hands of the Arabs. By contrast, al-Fadl ibn Sahl was of Persian origin and was also determined to ensure that al-Ma'mun, the son of a lower-class lady, ascended the Abbasid throne. If al-Ma'mun became the Abbasid Caliph, he obviously expected to be rewarded handsomely for his loyalty and support. Indeed, had it not been for al-Fadl ibn Sahl's loyalty, support and encouragement, al-Ma'mun might have surrendered his claim to the throne but, thanks to al-Fadl's persistence, he decided to fight for his right to ascend the Abbasid throne. By openly violating the deed of succession, Caliph al-Amin thus started a lengthy internal feud within the house of Harun al-Rashid.

As a result, al-Amin's reign became dominated by a war of slow destruction with his brother. Harun had placed the deed of succession in the *Haram al-Sharif* (the sacred mosque in Makkah) as a trust. But al-Amin had it brought to him and he tore it into pieces with his own hands. He then tried to remove al-Ma'mun from his post as governor of Khurasan. But al-Fadl ibn Sahl gathered sufficient public support for him so that he could openly challenge the Caliph's order and refuse to give up his governorship. In response, Caliph al-Amin sent a large army under the command of Ali ibn Isa to forcibly remove al-Ma'mun from power. However, the latter fought back and inflicted a crushing defeat on the Caliph's forces, firstly at Rayy and then at Hamadan.

Al-Ma'mun then captured Basrah and Kufah and also took the northern Iraqi city of Mosul. Soon afterwards, he was declared Caliph. Al-Amin, betrayed by his bodyguard, was captured and brutally murdered by the supporters of the new Caliph. His greed and jealousy led to his premature death at the age of only twenty-seven. So now the twenty-two-year-old al-Ma'mun ascended the Abbasid throne and went on to exert tremendous influence on the Muslim world.

Al-Ma'mun initially ruled from his headquarters in Merv. However, when political rebellion and social disorder broke out in different parts of the empire, and rebel groups and bandits began to wreak havoc across his dominion, he decided to return to Baghdad and boost his political and military authority. From having once been economically very prosperous and culturally advanced, Baghdad now lay in ruins. The war fought by the two brothers had brought this great city to its knees, turning most of Baghdad into rubble. This sorry situation moved and deeply saddened al-Ma'mun on his arrival in Baghdad. Thus, he went out of his way to mend broken relationships by reconciling himself with his previous opponents within the royal family.

He was keen to win the support of Zubaida, Caliph al-Amin's mother. So al-Ma'mun returned all her wealth and properties to her. After reuniting the royal family under his able leadership, he turned his attention to events outside the capital and initiated military actions to put an end to all the rebellious activities which were taking place within the Abbasid dominion at the time. The political situation had deteriorated so badly that many Abbasid territories, such as Tunisia, claimed their independence from Abbasid rule. But, thanks to al-Ma'mun's wise, timely and decisive actions, peace and security were soon restored across the Muslim world. He became the undisputed ruler of the Abbasid Empire.

As an educated and cultured ruler, al-Ma'mun was very fond of intellectual debates and discussions. He also established a Council of the State, comprising representatives from different regions of the empire. These regional representatives had a permanent seat at the Council and provided feedback on central government performance policies and programmes. Since al-Ma'mun was very keen to engage directly with his subjects, he considered the views of the regional representatives before deciding on the vital issues of the day. Being a great organiser and motivator of people, he also encouraged his generals to instil discipline and moral values within the ranks of his armed forces.

He was determined to stamp out corruption and dishonest practices from his government and armed services so he paid his senior civil servants and army generals handsomely. He also supplied them with all the necessary equipment, weaponry and training needed to perform their duties. He was especially generous towards his Ministers and Chief Advisor, al-Fadl ibn Sahl. Indeed, he authorised the latter to draw an annual salary of three million dirhams from the State coffers. Although this was an enormous sum, al-Ma'mun was keen to reward his staff handsomely to prevent corruption, bribery and malpractice from rearing their ugly heads within his government, and in this respect, he was very successful.

Like his father, al-Ma'mun transformed Baghdad into a thriving city. Under his stewardship, it became the world's most dazzling capital city, being renowned for its schools, colleges, hospitals, markets, bookshops and libraries. As a generous patron of learning and education, he transformed the *Bait al-Hikmah* (the House of Wisdom), which was originally founded by his father Caliph Harun al-Rashid, into one of the Muslim world's most famous libraries and research centres. He expanded its activities and renamed it *Dar al-Hikmah* (the Abode of Wisdom). He recruited some of the Muslim world's brightest minds, including al-Kindi (see chapter 35), al-Farghani, known in the West as Alfraganus, and al-Khwarizmi (see chapter 32), popularly known as 'Algorithm', to this centre of learning so they could pursue advanced research in science, philosophy, mathematics and literature.

Caliph al-Ma'mun ruled at a time when the Islamic world became polarised into two major philosophical and theological camps. Prominent religious scholars, like Imam Ahmad ibn Hanbal (see chapter 31), became the champions of Islamic traditionalism, while the rationalists became supporters of the Mu'tazilite creed. Though al-Ma'mun was well-versed in traditional Islamic sciences (having, according to some scholars, attended Malik ibn Anas's lectures in Madinah), he chose to champion the views of the Mu'tazilites. This resulted in Mu'tazilism becoming the official creed of the State during his reign.

As a ruler, al-Ma'mun was neither despotic nor tyrannical, others differ on this, but, as a champion of Mu'tazilism, he was both stubborn and uncompromising. When a controversy concerning the nature of the Qur'an flared up during his reign, he ruthlessly imposed his theological views on his opponents. The Islamic traditionalists argued that the Qur'an was *ghair makluq* (the uncreated word of Allah). Al-Ma'mun – like the Mu'tazilites –considered it to be a created Word of Allah. Anyone who preached against this was treated harshly by him. When Imam Ahmad ibn Hanbal, who was a leading Islamic theologian and scholar, opposed al-Ma'mun's religious views, he and his successors cruelly chastised him.

Al-Ma'mun's attitude and behaviour towards Imam Ahmad ibn Hanbal was both bizarre and mysterious because his reign as Caliph represented a great period of political stability, economic prosperity, intellectual progress and advancement across the Muslim world. The leading Mu'tazilite scholars were keen to teach the Islamic traditionalists a good lesson. So they encouraged al-Ma'mun to take a firm stance against their traditionalist opponents. Al-Ma'mun's action against the traditionalists was both foolish and unwise, not least because it tarnished and undermined his reputation as a wise and tolerant sovereign.

Caliph al-Ma'mun's reign of two and a half decades came to an end when he was forty-seven. He died in the village of Budandun (in present-day Pozanti, located in Adana, Turkey) during a military expedition he led against the Byzantines. Before his death, he reportedly confessed his theological errors and prayed for forgiveness. His body was transferred to Tarsus where he was laid to rest following a simple funeral. Unlike his father, al-Ma'mun left no instructions about political succession. As expected, his half-brother Muhammad, better known as al-Mu'tasim Bi'llah succeeded him as Caliph.

34

Fatimah al-Fihriyyah (b.ca.800 - d.880 CE) / (b.184 - d.267 AH)

Fatimah al-Fihriyyah was born in the ninth century in Kairouan, Tunisia. Her father, Muhammad bin Abdullah, was a merchant, and so she grew up in a privileged and educated home. When she was small, her father decided to migrate to Morocco with her and her sister. This happened during the rule of Idrees II who was an extraordinary ruler and devout Muslim.

They came to Fez, which at that time was a lively city of *al-Maghrib* (the Muslim West). It was known for having the potential for people's fortune and security. As one of the most influential Muslim cities, Fez was famous for its religion and culture as well. It had a traditional way, mainly due to the local inhabitants however, it was also diverse because people from other places would go there. Fatimah's family settled on the banks of the River Fez. Initially, the family struggled and experienced challenges with earning their livelihood. However, over time, they were blessed with success. Their father became a rich businessman and was well-respected in the community.

We do not know much about her personal life other than the fact that she was renowned for being a deep thinker. Her legacy, however, can be found in the memorable work she accomplished and the landmark she built. In around 859 CE, as a young lady, Fatimah al-Fihriyyah did something remarkable which stands out as a shining example in the records of history.

Her father was keen on educating his children who were taught at home, as was the tradition of the time for middle and upper-class women. Later, she married and lived as a devout and worshipful woman while supporting her family. Fatimah spent her time in study and charitable causes. Suddenly, her life changed when her husband, brother and father died within a short period. It is thought that she was in her fifties at the time.

This far-sighted woman set her vision on constructing what would become the main degree-awarding institution of her time. Since she belonged to a prestigious family, her father's early death left her with a large inheritance. Fatimah and her sister inherited his wealth which gave them financial stability. Both sisters wanted to make sure their inheritance turned into a long-lasting and beneficial legacy. After receiving a good education, both sisters turned their attention towards their community. Mariam, Fatimah's sister, observed that the local population and the Muslim refugees from Islamic Andalusia (modern Spain and Portugal) could not be accommodated in the mosques of Fez. To support them, she decided to build the magnificent Andalusian Mosque.

At the same time, Fatimah had her vision set on reforming education for others. She used the money from her inheritance to build a mosque and a *madrasah* where people could get authentic knowledge. She had realised early on that in the future, the *madrasah* and mosque would need to be extended. For this reason, she had bought the surrounding land and property adjacent to her first plot in advance. This decision is a testament to her high aspirations and foresight. Eventually, when the time came, she was able to increase the size of the complex. She carefully spent her time and money to see the projects completed. Historical accounts mention that she supervised, guided and project-managed the entire construction process by being there all the time. This shows her remarkable dedication and eagerness for quality and attention to detail.

As she was a moral and religious woman, another highly commendable action of hers was that she ensured that the building material only came from the land of the complex. They did not take any soil from another place to protect the sanctity of the mosque. All the materials and processes were completed in a *halal* (lawful)manner. Moreover, because of her devout religious conviction and piety, she started the project by fasting from the first day until its completion. However, it is more likely that she was particular about fasting regularly as a normal practice. When the building was completed some years later, she offered prayers of gratitude in the same mosque that she had so diligently worked to construct.

Overtime, al-Qarawiyyin enrolled hundreds of students. This resulted in many *madrassas* being commissioned and built in the area to accommodate students. Al-Qarawiyyin had now become a place of worship and a place of higher learning. At the same time, Fatimah also became known as the 'Mother of Children' because she often took care of students and supported their studies through grants.

After some years, the establishment grew to become The University and Mosque of al-Qarawiyyin, named after her place of birth in Tunisia, Kairouan. It became the first and largest mosque and university complex in North Africa, educating students from all over the world. During the medieval times, the University was considered a famous intellectual centre. As an educational centre, Al-Qarawiyyin was rooted in an ethos where people were aware of Allah. Their soul was purified and their minds were nurtured. The al-Qarawiyyin Mosque and University was not merely a religious institution but also a centre of learning. The curriculum was broad and consisted of Qur'an, Islamic theology, law, rhetoric, writing, logic, arithmetic, philosophy, geography, medicine, grammar, Muslim history, astronomy, chemistry and mathematics. Scientists and scholars from around the world arrived here to learn at this outstanding educational institution. In this way, Fatimah founded the world's first university in Fez, Morocco. The Qarawiyyin *madrasah* is a mosque and college complex renowned for being one of the oldest universities; currently, it is located in the ancient heart of the city.

Fatimah al-Fihriyyah's thirst for knowledge and learning was limitless. When she was fifty-nine, she enrolled herself in the university and graduated. Despite being the founder of such a prestigious educational institute and becoming a role model for many, she continued to gain knowledge.

Amongst those who graduated from the university are some of the most prominent Muslim scholars, including Ibn Khaldun (see chapter 75) and the Maliki jurist Ibn al-Arabi (see chapter 65). The University was also attended by non-Muslims. It is said that Christians, like Pope Sylvester II, were there. Some have mentioned that one of the University's most famous students was the great Jewish physician and philosopher, Maimonides. The University is also credited with producing many distinguished thinkers including Abu al-Abbas, the jurist Muhammad al-Fasi and Leo Africanus, the famous author, geographer and traveller. The fact that al-Qarawiyyin University produced scholars who influenced not only the Muslim world but also Europe and beyond speaks volumes about the trans-formative power of education across borders and cultures. Some suggest that Al-Qarawiyyin University came before the University of Bologna (circa. 1080) by approximately 100 years. The mosque is one of the most ancient in the world, dating back even further than the mosque in Timbuktu.

The historically rich and impressive library of al-Qarawiyyin University is one of the oldest in the world, claiming a similar title to the university itself. However, in 1323 CE, a fire ravaged and de-stroyed thousands of manuscripts held there, including many pri-mary sources and other documents. Nevertheless, it still has many attractions. It contains thousands of books and more than 4000 manuscripts including the famous historian Ibn Khaldun's four-teenth-century text *Muqaddimah*. It has also preserved valuable manuscripts from the *Muwatta* of Imam Malik (see chapter 24) and the *Sirah* of Ibn Ishaq (see chapter 23). It also houses a precious ninth-century copy of the Qur'an, written in ornate Kufic script on a parchment. Of the many historical treasures, one is Fatimah's orig-inal diploma written on a piece of wood, which is safely stored. After the Moroccan Ministry of Culture commissioned its rehabili-tation and curation, it was re-opened to the public in 2016.

The University is recognised by the United Nations Education, Scientific and Cultural Organisation (UNESCO) and the Guinness Book of Records as the first-degree granting university in the world. The building still exists in Morocco today.

Fatimah's biography shows that many women were educated in her time and were valued in society. Many were benefactors of mosques and charitable projects. The tradition of Muslim female scholarship begins with the advent of Islam (see chapter 12). Fatimah's story serves as a reminder that women have played pivotal roles in shaping history.

Al-Qarawiyyin University's enduring presence and its continuous commitment to education stand as a living tribute to Fatimah's vision and legacy. It is a symbol of history and culture for the region. Her impact has extended far beyond her time, influencing scholars, researchers and students for centuries. Her determination, foresight and courage broke down barriers and opened doors for future generations, thus showcasing that women can be leaders, innovators and influencers with the help of Allah. Over 1200 years have passed since the establishment of the University and it continues to graduate students in religious and physical sciences. The outstanding legacy of her dedication and empowering efforts is a source of inspiration for many today.

35

Al-Kindi
(b.801 - d.873 CE) / (b.185 - d.260 AH)

Some subjects, such as mathematics and biology, are more precise and better defined than other subjects like philosophy. Both mathematicians and biologists agree on what they want to study and explore, but that is not the case with the philosophers. The definition of philosophy is controversial and their different views which existed long ago within philosophical circles continue to this day.

The ancient Greek philosophers such as Socrates, Plato and Aristotle became great champions of philosophical thinking, but they did not pursue philosophy in a unified way. Their inspirational contribution to philosophical thought remained in misery for hundreds of years until the sun finally shone on Arabia in the seventh century. The Arabs were rescued from being a footnote of history by the Prophet Muhammad and because of him, they embraced learning, culture and civilisation like never before.

The early Muslim scholars and philosophers not only translated original Greek philosophical material into Arabic, but they also wrote detailed commentaries on them. They also refined the ideas of the ancient Greek philosophers. By doing this, they paved the way for the emergence of *falsafah* (Islamic philosophy). It was al-Kindi, that hugely influential Islamic philosopher - known in the West as the 'philosopher of the Arabs' (*faylasuf al-Arab*) - who played a central role in the development of philosophical thought in the Muslim world.

Yaqub ibn Ishaq al-Kindi, known in the Latin West as Alkindus, was born in Kufah, Iraq. He originated from the south Arabian tribe of Kindah. His grandfather, al-Ash'ath ibn Qais claimed to be a *Sahabi* (companion) of the Prophet Muhammad. His father, Ishaq ibn al-Sabbah, was a respected member of the Abbasid and served as governor of Kufah during the reign of Abbasid Caliphs al-Mahdi, al-Hadi and Harun al-Rashid. Along with Basrah, Baghdad, Damascus, Makkah and Madinah, Kufah was one of the foremost centres of Islamic learning at the time. He was brought up in a wealthy and learned family. Al-Kindi attended his local schools and studied Arabic language, grammar, literature and traditional Islamic sciences during his early years before specialising in Islamic theology, mathematics, astronomy and philosophy. As a gifted student, he excelled in his studies and was able to learn both the religious and philosophical sciences of his day with ease.

After completing his formal education in Kufah, al-Kindi moved to Baghdad, the political capital of the Islamic world, to pursue advanced training in the religious and philosophical sciences. After the death of Harun al-Rashid, his son al-Ma'mun (see chapter 33) became the Caliph and enthusiastically promoted the study of the rational sciences, including Greek philosophy and science, across the Muslim world. This created an intellectually friendly atmosphere for Muslim scientists and philosophers to conduct their research into scientific, philosophical and religious subjects. In Baghdad, al-Kindi enjoyed the sponsorship of Caliph al-Ma'mun, who encouraged him to pursue his studies at the *Bait al-Hikmah* (House of Wisdom), the celebrated library and research centre originally founded by Harun al-Rashid. In it, some of the leading Muslim philosophers and scientists of the day pursued their research into their chosen areas of specialisation. At the *Bait al-Hikmah*, al-Kindi devoted all his time and energy to the study of mathematics, astronomy, chemistry, musical theory and philosophy. During this period, he earned his livelihood working as a calligrapher at the Caliphal court in Baghdad.

Along with other celebrities of the time, including al-Khwarizmi (see chapter 32) the great mathematician, and al-Farghani, the renowned astronomer, al-Kindi became an important member of the *Bait al-Hikmah*. Together they transformed this institute into one of the most famous centres of academic study and research in the Muslim world at the time. Though some of the theological and philosophical views of these intellectuals were considered to be controversial by traditionalist scholars such as Imam Ahmad ibn Hanbal (see chapter 31), Caliph al-Ma'mun gave them his full support and encouraged them to continue their intellectual activities.

Caliph al-Ma'mun became very fond of al-Kindi due to his intellectual brilliance and great linguistic abilities. So he asked him to lead the innovative task of translating Greek, Persian and Indian philosophical, mathematical and scientific works into Arabic for the benefit of Muslim scholars and researchers. Al-Kindi was appointed head of a team of dedicated scholars who conducted extensive research into comparative thought. He was appointed as the head because he was a talented linguist and an expert in ancient Indian, Greek and Persian philosophy and thought. They translated and edited a large quantity of ancient philosophical and scientific literature into Arabic for the very first time. Thanks to al-Kindi and his colleagues, the study of comparative thought became one of the main intellectual activities of the early Muslim philosophers and scientists.

Al-Kindi was Caliph al-Ma'mun's favourite intellectual, he not only translated philosophical and scientific works from ancient languages and undertook research in almost all the branches of learning known during his time, but was also later chosen by Caliph Mu'tasim Bi'llah to teach and guide his son. The new Caliph held him in very high esteem for his valuable contribution to learning and research. Al-Kindi was appointed chief astrologer at the Caliphal court in Baghdad when he was only thirty-two years old. He was blessed with a powerful memory and an encyclopaedic mind. He excelled in a wide range of subjects including mathematics, astronomy, physics, chemistry, astrology, music, optics, geography, religious sciences, comparative thought and literature. However, it was in the fields of optics, music and philosophy that he made some of his most original contributions.

For the first time in the history of optics, al-Kindi fully explained the principle of rectilinear progress of light emerging from a shining object. As one of the most fundamental principles of optics, this is common knowledge today, but back in the ninth century, it was one of the most remarkable discoveries ever made in this field because he was able to prove his theory by conducting experiments. Using a lit candle, hence becoming known as the 'candle experiment', al-Kindi was able to demonstrate that light progressed in a straight line. Furthermore, his books on geometrical and physiological optics were so accurate and advanced for the time that they subsequently became standard works of reference in optical science both in the East and the West.

His contribution to the field of musical theory was equally remarkable. He was widely considered to be one of the greatest musical theorists in history. He penned seven books and essays on the subject. According to historians, he was one of the first to write on music and musical theory and as such should be considered the father of this branch of learning. In his writings, al-Kindi explained in considerable detail the meaning and significance of rhythm, especially focusing on its role in classical Arab music; Since musical songs formed an important part of Arab culture, he was keen to develop a theoretical understanding of music – a branch of learning that the Muslims later exported to the West. Without al-Kindi's original contribution in this field, the world of music would certainly have been much poorer in its understanding and appreciation of the aesthetic dimension of music.

Al-Kindi's contributions to optics and musical theory were remarkable. But today he is most famous for his philosophical originality and writings. He authored twenty- two books on philosophy. He became a towering figure in this subject both in the Muslim world and in the West, where he became widely known as the 'philosopher of the Arabs' as a result of his huge influence on Western philosophers and thinkers. In his famous book, *Fi al-falsafah al-ula* (On First Philosophy), he defined philosophy as 'the knowledge of the nature of things in so far as this is possible for man. The aim of the philosopher is, as regards his knowledge, to attain to the truth, and as regards his action, to act truthfully.'

To al-Kindi, philosophy consisted of three parts, ranked in order of importance: theology, mathematics and physics. By lifting theology to the highest point in philosophical discussion, he experienced the wrath of the traditional religious scholars. They argued that rational thinking on matters of religious beliefs was nothing short of heresy. Al-Kindi, however, disagreed with the traditionalists.

He was far from being a heretic, as some claimed. Indeed, he remained a sincere and committed Muslim who practised traditional Islamic teachings both in public and in private. However, unlike the traditionalists, his faithfulness to Islam did not prevent him from learning and championing ancient Greek philosophical thought. He frequently expressed his admiration for Plato and Aristotle – being the first and only great Arab philosopher to do so – but he did not compromise his Islamic faith and beliefs in the process. He remained a committed Muslim all his life.

The traditional religious scholars of his time considered religion and philosophy to be incompatible. Al-Kindi strongly disagreed with this view. He considered religion and philosophy to be compatible in the same way that reason and revelation are agreeable. In his philosophical works, he thoroughly analysed and dissected Greek philosophical thought from an Islamic perspective to reconcile classical Greek philosophy with the Qur'anic worldview. His attempts to harmonise the two perspectives proved so successful that they paved the way for the emergence of a separate Islamic philosophical tradition.

As a philosopher, al-Kindi did not discover or introduce a new principle in philosophical thinking. Rather his originality lay in the fact that he was able to survey the Greek philosophical tradition through the philosophical lens of Islam. In his definition of philosophy, al-Kindi identified two components which formed the foundation of his philosophical discussion. These were 'true knowledge' and 'true action'. The connection between knowledge and action was highly significant for al-Kindi because philosophy and the practical ethics of Islam were, in his opinion, interconnected both at a theoretical level and in the daily affairs of the Muslims.

According to al-Kindi, philosophy relates to the nature of God, Divine Attributes, creation and time. The classical Greek philosophers, particularly the Aristotelian idea of God as the unmoved mover of all, was similar to the Islamic conception of Divinity. The Qur'an says Allah is One and created everything. Therefore, al-Kindi had no problems in accepting the Greek view on this matter. Unlike many other great Muslim philosophers, such as Ibn Sina, he believed that creation was not eternal. He considered time, space and the chain of causality to be finite and limited. Only God was infinite, he argued, because He was the first cause which was not an effect. He also insisted that the human body would be resurrected according to Islamic teachings. He was a firm believer in *al-qada' wal-qadr* (universal Divine Providence).

He was quick to point out that perfect order and harmony in creation was a further sign of the existence of Allah. Al-Ghazali later thoroughly discredited the teleological argument for the existence of Allah. Nevertheless, al-Kindi's translations, extensive commentaries and his mixture of Islamic thought with the Greek worldview opened the way for famous Muslim philosophers and thinkers like al-Farabi (see chapter 41), Abu Bakr al-Razi (see chapter 39), Ibn Sina (see chapter 52), al-Ghazali (see chapter 56), Ibn Bajjah, Ibn Tufayl and Ibn Rushd (see chapter 60) to emerge and present a more comprehensive Islamic philosophical position.

According to the well-known bibliographer al-Nadim, al-Kindi authored exactly two hundred and forty-two books and essays on all the sciences of his day. But, according to others, he wrote two hundred and eighty works. Either way, the vast majority of al-Kindi's books are no longer in existence. Nevertheless, historians agree that he was a truly great philosopher, encyclopaedist and prolific writer. His achievements were so wide-ranging that influential European thinkers like Roger Bacon considered him to be one of the world's greatest minds. After a number of his books were translated into Latin by Gerard of Cremona. Al-Kindi became popular in the West as a philosopher and optician. In the Muslim world, he became known as the 'father of Islamic philosophy'.

As an enthusiastic champion of philosophy and scientific thought, al-Kindi suffered persecution at the hands of the traditionally minded Caliph Mutawakkil 'ala Allah who, after ascending the Abbasid throne, drove out the philosophical rationalists from the Caliphal court in Baghdad. Ironically, al-Kindi survived his tormentor by more than a decade and died at the age of seventy-two.

36

Al-Bukhari
(b.810 - d.870 CE) / (b.194 - 257 d.AH)

The life and teachings of the Prophet Muhammad are an important source of inspiration, guidance and instruction for more than a billion Muslims across the globe today. A Muslim can draw direct guidance for all spheres of his life from the vast *Hadith* literature. This includes how to conduct a multi-billion-pound business transaction in the international marketplace to the finer details of how to drink a glass of water. The Arabic word *Hadith* refers to a 'saying' of the Prophet. No other human being is followed as closely as the Prophet is followed by the Muslims. He is seen as the height of virtue, goodness and humanity. That is why Muslims thoroughly copy his *Sunnah* (actions) in everything they do. In Islamic history, one man stands over and above all others when it comes to collecting, editing, analysing and verifying the sayings of the Prophet. He is none other than Imam al-Bukhari.

Muhammad ibn Isma'il al-Bukhari was born in Bukhara, in Muslim Central Asia, in modern Uzbekistan. He was of Persian origin. Imam al-Bukhari's ancestors were farmers. His father, Isma'il, was a relatively wealthy merchant and an expert scholar of *Hadith*. He was well known in his locality for his good habits and strict following of the practice of the Prophet. He had two sons, Ahmad and Muhammad. Muhammad was the younger son and became well known as Imam al-Bukhari. Isma'il died when al-Bukhari was still a child, and the family fell into poverty and hardship. But young al-Bukhari's mother was a pious and determined lady who, despite her difficult economic circumstances, ensured her son received a good education.

Al-Bukhari was a gifted student who possessed a photographic memory and great analytical skills. Of slim build and somewhat frail health, he still excelled in his studies. His ability to grasp complex arguments and resolve opposing views —elevated him to one of the highest positions ever to be attained by a scholar of *Hadith*. He had an extraordinary intellect and unusual memory power. Al-Bukhari's love for Islamic learning, especially his search for Prophetic traditions, became very evident early in his life. It was his devoted mother who played a critical role in his early education. She inspired him to pursue the study of *Hadith*.

After completing his initial education at the age of twelve, al-Bukhari continued with advanced training in Islamic sciences and specialised in *Hadith* literature. His hard work and dedication to his studies paid off when he completed his study of *Hadith* under the guidance of all the reputable scholars of Bukhara. He was only eighteen at the time. In fact, he was barely twenty when he came to be recognised as one of the top scholars of *Hadith* in his locality. Thereafter, the study, collection and verification of Prophetic traditions became his lifelong mission. It was this which established his reputation as one of Islam's greatest authorities on *Hadith*. The signs of his greatness were evident from the very outset. It is related that when al-Bukhari was only eleven, he once corrected his own teacher's mistake. When the teacher refused to take him seriously, al-Bukhari challenged him to check his facts. After the teacher checked his manuscript, al-Bukhari was found to be correct.

After completing his higher education in Bukhara, Imam al-Bukhari left his native city and went to Makkah, along with his mother and brother, to perform the sacred *hajj*. He stayed in Makkah and Madinah for several years and gained advanced training in *Hadith* literature under the guidance of the leading scholars of the time. From Makkah, he travelled to other great centres of Islamic learning in Egypt, Syria and Iraq before settling in Basrah for further research in *Hadith*. Like many other great scholars of his era, al-Bukhari was a distinguished traveller who spent nearly four decades journeying from one place to another in search of knowledge and wisdom.

These celebrated scholars of *Hadith* played a crucial role in the development of *ulum al-Hadith* (the science of *Hadith*). Al-Bukhari was a master at sifting and distinguishing the authentic *Hadith* from the fabricated ones. He did this by cross-examining every *Hadith* from multiple perspectives to establish the authenticity of the *matn* (text) of the *Hadith*; its chains of *isnad* (narration), the background of *al asma al rijal* (the Hadith narrator), as well as sound knowledge and understanding of the Qur'an to determine whether the *Hadith* complied with the Divine revelation.

After systematic investigations of the *ahadith*, the *muhaddithun* (scholars of *Hadith*) classified them into different categories such as *sahih* (sound), *hasan* (good), *daeef* (weak), *maudu* (fabricated) and so on. However, given the fact that the quantity of *Hadith* which were in circulation during al-Bukhari's time was incredibly vast, so sifting through them became a monumental task even for a gifted scholar like al-Bukhari. Nonetheless, his incredible mind power enabled him to memorise around half a million *Hadith*. This established his reputation as a master of *Hadith* lliterature and his fame spread across the Islamic East. After four decades of nonstop quest for knowledge, al-Bukhari reached the summit of Islamic scholarship. A lofty position which no other scholar of *Hadith* was able to rival after him.

For Imam al-Bukhari, learning, collecting and spreading *Hadith* became a way of life. He travelled to distant lands and sacrificed all his time, energy and wealth in the pursuit of Prophetic *Hadith*. He was also a man of impeccable character, piety and honourable manners and habits. He ate most sparingly and led a very simple lifestyle. He followed in the steps of the Prophet whose sayings and utterances he was so eager to preserve for later generations. He became so well in *Hadith* literature that on several occasions, he allowed his knowledge of *Hadith* to be tested by some of the most distinguished scholars of his time. During one such occasion, ten reputable scholars of Baghdad publicly put him to the test to find out his knowledge of Prophetic traditions.

They deliberately changed the chain of *isnad* (narration) of around one hundred different *ahadith*, and then recited them to him in front of the public. He was then asked to comment on them. Al-Bukhari confessed that he was not familiar with those *ahadith*. He then recited all the authentic versions of the same *Hadith* with their correct chains of narration. He then commented that the scholars who had recited the hundred *ahadith* might have confused their chains of narration. Al-Bukhari's depth and breadth of learning left his interrogators, as well as the spectators, utterly spellbound. In short, al-Bukhari emerged from such tests with his reputation enhanced.

If Imam al-Bukhari was a great master and memoriser of *Hadith*, then he was an equally prolific writer. After collecting more than half a million *Hadith*, he systematically examined them to ascertain their authenticity. Thereafter, he classified all the *Hadith* according to a grading scale, thus sifting the sound traditions from the fabricated ones. Such a scientific method, developed by al-Bukhari and his contemporaries, enabled him to collect and preserve only the authentic Prophetic traditions for the benefit of future generations. It is also worth highlighting that al-Bukhari began to write books from an early age. He composed his first book on *Hadith* during his stay in Madinah, when he was only eighteen. This book contained a large collection of sayings attributed to the Prophet's Sahabah (companions) and their *tabiun* (successors).

In other words, his intellectual and literary achievements during his student days were remarkable. All his teachers praised his intellectual abilities and vast learning. Some even predicted a bright future for him. As it happened, he contributed more to Islamic thought and scholarship than any other scholar of his generation. His collection of *Hadith* in short is known as *Sahih al-Bukhari* and is today widely considered to be the most authentic book of Islamic teachings after the Holy Qur'an. Using strict criteria, to establish the genuineness of every *Hadith*, he sifted through more than half a million *ahadith* and chose only the most authentic ones for inclusion in his *Jami al-Sahih*. He completed his treasure of *Hadith* after almost four decades of research.

Jami al-Sahih consists of more than seven thousand and two hundred Prophetic narrations. This collection of *Hadith* has established al-Bukhari's reputation as one of the Muslim world's most famous and influential scholars. *Jami al-Sahih* represents the peak of achievement in the field of *Hadith* literature. It is very unlikely that another scholar of al-Bukhari's calibre will appear again.

After decades of travelling in the single-minded pursuit of Islamic knowledge and wisdom, al-Bukhari returned to Muslim Central Asia and settled in Nishapur. He was fifty-four at the time. The people of that city received him warmly. He continued to study, research and teach Prophetic traditions until the local governor forced him to leave the city for refusing to deliver lectures on *Hadith* at his official residence. Imam al-Bukhari then settled in a small town adjacent to his native Bukhara and passed away at the age of approximately sixty.

37

Muslim ibn al-Hajjaj
(b.817 - d.875 CE) / (b.202 - d.262 AH)

Islamic history is filled with great *muhaddithun* (scholars of *Hadith*) who received extensive approval for their brilliant contributions in the field of *Hadith*. Thus, scholars like Malik ibn Anas (see chapter 24), Imam al-Zuhri, Imam al-Awza'i and Abdullah ibn Mubarak have left their permanent marks in the history of *Hadith* literature. Thanks to them, the preservation and spreading of *Hadith* and *usul al-hadith* (the science of *Hadith*) became possible and made them the most popular subjects of the *ulum al-din* (traditional Islamic sciences).

However, the names of two remarkable scholars, al-Bukhari (see chapter 36) and Muslim, have today become household names across the Muslim world on account of their selfless devotion, hardworking scholarship and inspirational contributions to the collection and distribution of the Prophetic traditions. Although al-Bukhari is widely considered to be the most famous scholar in the history of *Hadith* literature, the popularity of Muslim ibn al-Hajjaj must not be underestimated. In fact, according to some scholars of *Hadith*, Muslim's anthology of *Hadith* is superior to that of al-Bukhari. Nevertheless, the collections of both Imam al-Bukhari and Imam Muslim are today regarded as two of the most authentic and authoritative collections of Prophetic traditions ever produced. For this reason, both al-Bukhari and Muslim have been rated very highly in this book.

Muslim ibn al-Hajjaj was born in Nishabur which is in the Persian province of Khurasan. He was from a highly respected Arab family of the tribe Qushayr. His ancestors included people who had all played leading roles within the Islamic State during the time of the Prophet and the *al-khulafa al-rashidun* (the four rightly guided Caliphs). Following the rapid expansion of Islam during the reign of Caliphs Umar (see chapter 6) and Uthman (see chapter 4), Muslims began to move from Arabia and settle in the newly conquered territories in Syria, Egypt and Persia. They had businesses and also engaged in missionary activities. It was during this period that Muslim's ancestors left Arabia and settled in Nishabur.

As an outstanding scholar of Islam and respected authority on *Hadith* literature, his father taught him Arabic, the Qur'an, *Hadith* and fiqh (jurisprudence). He was raised in a family where the Prophetic traditions were admired and rigorously followed. So young Muslim became fond of *Hadith* literature from an early age. He was blessed with an intelligent mind and highly retentive memory. It did not take him long to acquire proficiency in Arabic language, grammar and aspects of traditional Islamic sciences. A thorough study of Arabic language and grammar was required for advanced training in the Qur'an and *Hadith*. That is why Muslim's father ensured his son acquired all the linguistic skills necessary to carry out such a task. Indeed, it was his father's great respect and admiration for the Prophetic traditions which inspired his son, Muslim, to specialise in *Hadith* literature.

He began his advanced training in *Hadith* at the age of fifteen. After completing a further study of *Hadith* sciences under the guidance of some of Nishabur's leading scholars, he went to Makkah to perform the hajj. During his stay in Makkah, he attended the lectures of some of the city's prominent scholars before he eventually returned home to Nishabur. Here, he soon encountered the celebrated Imam al-Bukhari whom he was delighted to meet. Although he was only a few years younger than al-Bukhari, by then he had also become widely respected in and around Nishabur for his wide knowledge of Prophetic traditions. According to historians, when al-Bukhari met Muslim, Muslim stood up and kissed the former on his forehead, saying, 'Let me kiss your feet, O master of

Hadith scholars and specialists in Prophetic traditions'. Thereafter, Muslims studied *Hadith* under al-Bukhari's instruction for a period and polished his knowledge and understanding of *Hadith* and usul al-*hadith*.

He was still eager to learn more. So, at the age of thirty-three, he travelled to some of the leading centres of Islamic learning in Persia, Iraq, Arabia, Syria and Egypt, and dedicated yet more time to the study of *Hadith*. This enabled him to learn more Prophetic traditions and master the art of investigating and separating the sound *Hadith* from the weak and doubtful ones. In those days, *rihla* (travel) from one place of learning to another was a necessity. It was a fundamental requirement for all true seekers of knowledge - especially if they wished to receive advanced training in any branch of Islamic learning. This was because most of the celebrated scholars of the time lived in different parts of the Muslim world. Thus, students like al-Bukhari, Muslim and others had no choice but to travel extensively in search of knowledge. In the process, they met with and studied *Hadith* under the guidance of hundreds of distinguished scholars and *Hadith* traditionalists of their time.

Some of Muslim's prominent teachers included Ishaq ibn Rahwayh, Imam Ahmad ibn Hanbal (see chapter 31), Yahya ibn Ma'in, Sa'id ibn Mansur and many others. These scholars were not only great authorities on *Hadith* literature, but they were also the original creators of the science of *Hadith*. Muslim sat at the feet of these luminaries and learned Prophetic traditions until he also became an outstanding authority in *Hadith* literature. When he was convinced that he had acquired an unrivalled mastery of Prophetic traditions, he returned home to Nishabur. Here his fame began to spread far and wide because of his deep knowledge and expertise in *Hadith* literature. Indeed, he became such a popular tutor that, during his lifetime, he was acknowledged as a great authority on Prophetic traditions along with Imam al-Bukhari and Imam al-Darimi of Samarqand. But in Nishabur he had no rivals. Here he was honoured more than any other scholar of his generation.

If Muslim was an Islamic scholar and traditionist of the highest standard, then he was also a man of great character and personality. He loved simplicity and openness and followed these principles very rigorously. As a true seeker of knowledge and wisdom, Muslim did not believe in intellectual rivalry or personal hatred. He followed the Prophetic traditions to the letter and even refused to criticise or speak unfavourably of others.

He earned his livelihood from his small family business. In his spare time, he delivered lectures on *Hadith*. His lectures became so popular that hundreds of students came from far afield to listen to him. Famous scholars like Imam al-Tirmidhi and Ibn Khuzaymah also attended his lectures. He was considered to have been one of the most pious and upright Islamic scholars of his generation. Imam Muslim was a great admirer of the Prophet. He authored scores of books on *Hadith*, *usul al-hadith*, *asma al-rijal* (biographies of *Hadith* narrators) and aspects of Islamic history.

He composed more than twenty books on different aspects of *Hadith*. But only six of his books have survived, including *al-Jami al-Sahih* (better known as *Sahih Muslim*). This collection of *Hadith* is not only his most famous work but, along with *Sahih al-Bukhari*, it is today considered to be one of the most authentic books of Islamic teachings after the Qur'an itself. It is honoured as one of the great works of traditional Islamic learning. The importance and relevance of this vast collection of Prophetic traditions cannot be emphasised enough. After fifteen years of thorough research and investigation in the field of *Hadith* (which involved examining through hundreds of thousands of Prophetic traditions to separate the authentic narrations from the weak or fabricated ones), Muslim incorporated around seven thousand a*hadith* in his anthology.

Muslim was an inventor of Islamic learning and helped to develop and spread a rigorous research method in the field of *Hadith* literature. He classified *Hadith* narrators into three broad categories. The first category consisted of narrators who possessed a highly retentive memory because they maintained consistency in their narrations. This enabled Muslim to compare their narrations with those of other respected and reliable narrators to establish their authenticity. The vast majority of *Hadith* contained in *Sahih Muslim* falls into this category. By contrast, the second category consisted of those narrators who had weak memories. Thus, their narrations were occasionally found to be inconsistent. Muslim accepted their narrations only if their versions of *Hadith* agreed with the narrations of the first category. On the other hand, the third category consisted of those narrators who were considered to be unreliable and untrustworthy. Imam Muslim completely rejected their narrations.

By using such an accurate system of checks and counterchecks, he successfully sifted the *sahih* (authentic) traditions from *hasan* (good) and the *daeef* (weak) from the *maudu* (fabricated). In doing so he produced a collection of Prophetic *Hadith* which today enjoys the full support and confidence of the Muslim community. Also, a reader of *Sahih Muslim* will notice how different versions of the same *Hadith* repeat themselves. This is because Muslim deliberately included a second version of the first *Hadith* to reinforce the message of the first narration.

The rigorous research method formulated by Muslim and his peers not only enabled them to check and re-check the authenticity of all the *Hadith* they collected, but it also served another important purpose: for a *Hadith* to be considered beyond blame, it had to have a sound *matn* (text) as well as a sound *isnad* (chain of narration), among other things. Thus, for instance, if the *isnad* of a narration was considered to be reliable but its *matn* was found to be illogical or contradictory, then that narration was classified as 'unreliable'. On the other hand, if the *matn* of a narration was considered to be sound but its *isnad* was found to be defective, then that narration was also considered to be 'unreliable'. However, if a particular *Hadith* reached Muslim through more than one *sanad* (chain of narration), he incorporated the narration with a weaker *isnad* (which contained a narrator with a weak memory) as confirmation of the first narration, because the latter had met all his strict tests.

Of the seven thousand Prophetic traditions he included in his *Jami al-Sahih*, four thousand belonged to the first category, while the remaining three thousand fell into the second category. This two-fold strategy employed by Muslim ensured his anthology contained only the most authentic narrations. After completing this huge work, he presented copies to some of his great contemporaries, including Abu Zur'ah of Rayy. After thoroughly checking the book, they all confirmed that it contained authentic Prophetic traditions. According to some scholars of *Hadith*, *Sahih Muslim* is one of the most authoritative anthologies of *Hadith* ever produced. This is because, unlike many other compilers of *Hadith*, Muslim appears not to have made any mistakes in the *isnad* (chain of narration) or the *matn* (text) of the traditions he included in his *Sahih*.

Not surprisingly, his anthology is today considered to be one of the two most important collections of *Hadith*, along with that of al-Bukhari. That is why so many famous scholars have written commentaries on *Sahih Muslim*, including the influential Syrian scholar al-Nawawi (see chapter 71). As the *Sahih Muslim* is rated very highly as a source of Islamic teachings, it would not be an exaggeration to say that the world of traditional Islamic learning and scholarship would have been much poorer without this great anthology. Imam Muslim ibn al-Hajjaj died at the age of only about fifty-nine. He was buried in his local city of Nishabur. But his name and fame will continue to live for a long time.

38

Al-Tabari
(b.839 - d.923 CE) / (b.223 - d.311AH)

The pre-Islamic Arabs became famous for preserving and transmitting historical and ancestral information from one generation to another through oral communication. After the emergence of Islam in Arabia, the Arabs – for the first time in their history – embraced learning and education with much interest and enthusiasm. And One subject in which the early Muslims excelled more than any other was history. But that was not too surprising because a large portion of the Qur'an consisted of historical information and data about the ancient people and their activities. The study of history thus became one of the foremost interests of the early Muslim scholars, thinkers and writers.

Ibn Khaldun is today widely considered to be the most influential Muslim historian of all time because of his profound originality and continued influence on the development of modern social sciences and the study of history. But the coveted title of 'father of Islamic history' has rightly been awarded to al-Tabari for his monumental contribution to Islamic historiography. Indeed, he is today considered to be one of the Muslim world's most influential historians and Qur'anic commentators.

Muhammad ibn Jarir al-Tabari was born in Amul in the Persian territory of Tabaristan, now in eastern Azerbaijan. His father was a wealthy Persian businessman who ensured his son received the best education that money could buy. After learning Arabic and Persian, young al-Tabari successfully committed the entire Qur'an to memory when he was only seven. He then studied Arabic literature and traditional Islamic sciences. As a talented child, he completed his early education while he was still in his teens. Encouraged and financed by his wealthy family, he then moved to the historic Persian city of Rayy to pursue further education.

Unlike Amul, Rayy was a flourishing centre of Islamic learning and commercial activity. Here he attended the lectures of the city's leading scholars and became thoroughly familiar with Arabic, Persian, *tafsir* (Qur'anic commentary), *Hadith*, *fiqh* (*Islamic jurisprudence*) and *ta'rikh* (history). As a true seeker of knowledge and wisdom, he preferred to read and study, rather than play games or engage in other worldly activities during his early years. Impressed with his son's remarkable intellectual ability and scholarly attitude, his father encouraged him to pursue higher education rather than join the family business.

Supported financially by his wealthy father, al-Tabari dedicated himself to his studies and read books and treatises on all aspects of traditional Islamic sciences. He read passionately during the night and attended the lectures of the local scholars during the day until he completed his formal education. Blessed with a highly retentive memory and a keen intellect, he was able to understand vast quantities of information with ease and outperformed many of his peers. From Rayy he went to Baghdad, the capital of the Abbasid Empire, to study under the guidance of the famous Imam Ahmad ibn Hanbal (see chapter 31). But when he arrived in Baghdad, at the age of twenty, he discovered that Ahmad ibn Hanbal had already passed away. After touring the city and having also attended the lectures of some of its leading scholars, he moved to Basrah and eventually settled in Kufah. He was shocked and dismayed by the political disorder and confusion which happened after the murder of Abbasid Caliph Mutawakkil 'ala Allah by his Turkish bodyguard. The quiet, peaceful and studious al-Tabari left Kufah and moved to Syria.

During this period, he lost contact with his family and began to experience considerable financial hardship and personal suffering. Although his father had left behind considerable wealth and assets back in his native Tabaristan, al-Tabari was unable to obtain any financial support. However, as a firm believer in the traditional Islamic saying that 'a luxurious lifestyle and learning do not go hand in hand', he suffered all the financial difficulties and personal hardships with great resilience and fortitude. Indeed, during this period he was forced to go without any proper meals, surviving on biscuits and water only. In desperation, he once sold the sleeves of his shirt to buy breadcrumbs for a meal. Despite suffering much pain and hardship, his stay in Syria proved very rewarding as he devoted all his time to the study of *Hadith*.

In fact, during this period he memorised a large number of Prophetic traditions, collected information about the life and times of the Prophet, and became thoroughly familiar with the views and opinions of the Prophet's *Sahabah* (companions) on all aspects of Islam. He lived at a time when travelling in search of knowledge was essential for all true seekers of wisdom. That was the only way a student could attend the lectures of all the leading scholars of the day where they lived and taught in important centres of Islamic learning like Makkah, Madinah, Baghdad, Basrah, Kufah and Damascus. As expected, al-Tabari travelled extensively in pursuit of knowledge and studied in Damascus, Makkah and Egypt, before finally returning to Baghdad.

After completing his advanced education, he began to teach and soon his name began to spread across Baghdad, thanks to his deep knowledge and understanding of Islam. He was a strict follower of the Prophetic *Sunnah* but he never married and remained a bachelor all his life. Instead, he devoted his entire life to learning and spreading Islamic knowledge and later became one of the most influential Islamic scholars of all time. When al-Tabari's reputation as a prominent Islamic scholar reached the corridors of power, the ruling Abbasid elites offered him well-paid government posts. But he politely declined their offers, preferring to live simply and continue his study and research into all the branches of Islamic learning.

He led a modest, pious and simple lifestyle and deliberately avoided the wealth and luxuries of this world, remaining totally focused on his intellectual pursuits. This was a remarkable achievement because, at the time, the forces of materialism and pleasure-seeking had entered the governmental circles in Baghdad and had also penetrated the ranks of the religious scholars. But al-Tabari, who was now widely considered to be a master of *Hadith*, *fiqh*, *tafsir* and Islamic history, remained totally detached. More importantly, his achievements in these Islamic subjects were nothing short of breathtaking.

As a jurist, he initially followed the school of Abu Hanifah (see chapter 21) but, after carrying out a thorough and systematic study of *Maliki*, *Shafi'i* and *Hanbali fiqh*, he became a follower of *hafi'i* jurisprudence. He followed the *Shafi'i madhhab* (see chapter 30) for nearly a decade before he developed his own interpretation of Islamic jurisprudence. Al-Tabari's understanding of *fiqh* was both complex and remarkably fluid and, as such, he continued to develop his thoughts on juristic matters right to the end of his life. Based on his interpretation of Islamic jurisprudence, a different school of Islamic legal thought known as the *Jariri madhhab* later emerged in the Muslim world. This *madhhab* initially claimed a sizeable following, but it subsequently died away. Since al-Tabari was thoroughly acquainted with all the prominent schools of Islamic jurisprudence, his ideas were variously influenced by all of them. Not surprisingly, his *madhhab* reflected the views of the *Hanafi*, *Shafi'i* and *Hanbali* jurists as much as it reflected his views. Having said that, al-Tabari was an outstanding jurist in his own right and his contribution to the field of Islamic jurisprudence was considerable.

Yet it is true that al-Tabari is today most famous for his contribution to the field of *tafsir*. After travelling far and wide, he collected a large quantity of information about the Qur'an, its history and methods of interpretation, and thus he became thoroughly familiar with all aspects of *tafsir* (Qur'anic sciences and commentary). He was in his sixties when he vowed to write two large books: one on the Qur'an and the other on history. As a scholar and writer of truly amazing energy, he used to study round the clock and wrote more than twenty pages daily for around forty years. Although these figures may be somewhat exaggerated, the fact that al-Tabari was an unusually prolific writer is not in doubt. The *Jami al-Bayan fi Tafsir al-Qur'an* (The Exhaustive Commentary on the Qur'an) is his Qur'anic commentary consisting of more than three thousand pages and was published in thirty bulky volumes.

Also known as *Tafsir-i-Tabari* (al-Tabari's Commentary), this book is not only a treasure trove of information about the Qur'an, its history, meaning and interpretation, but it is also one of the largest commentaries ever written on the Qur'an. Not surprisingly, *ulama* (Islamic scholars) and *mufassirun* (Qur'anic commentators) have continued to use it as a standard work of reference on *tafsir* to this day. All the great Qur'anic commentators such as al-Qurtubi, ibn Kathir, al-Zamakhshari, Fakhr al-Din al-Razi (see chapter 63), al-Suyuti, al-Baydawi and al-Alusi were profoundly influenced by al-Tabari's monumental *tafsir*.

As a commentator on the Qur'an, al-Tabari was a strict traditionalist who relied entirely on the Prophetic traditions, the views and opinions of the Prophet's *Sahabah* (companions) and those of their *tabiun* (successors) to explain the message of the Qur'an, rather than use his own rational decisions. For this reason, his commentary of the Qur'an is a *tafsir bi'l riwaya* or a commentary by way of transmission of Prophetic traditions through the mechanism of *isnad* (chain of narration). Nevertheless, he has been criticised by some Qur'anic commentators for incorporating information into his commentary without sifting the wheat from the chaff. For example, he has included the material of *isra'iliyat* (questionable data of Jewish origin) in his commentary. Then again, it is not surprising that some questionable data or information had crept into his commentary, given the voluminous nature of the work.

But, overall, al-Tabari's commentary is nothing short of a remarkable contribution to the field of *tafsir*. In fact, had it not been for his splendid efforts, the world of Qur'anic scholarship would have been deprived of a great treasure trove of information and data. If al-Tabari's *tafsir* was an invaluable contribution, then his *Kitab Ta'rikh al-Rusul wa'l Muluk* (The Book of the History of Prophets and Kings) must be considered one of the greatest works of history ever written. When he decided to write this voluminous work, he reportedly asked his friends whether they would be interested in reading a book on history. When his friends asked him how big it would be, he said it would be around sixty thousand pages long. The sheer size of the book prompted his friends to reply that they could not hope to finish such a large book. Al-Tabari was disappointed by his friends' remarks and felt the people of Baghdad no longer had any aspirations or ambitions.

He was not discouraged by his friends' apparent reluctance to read so he went on to compose his monumental *Kitab Tarikh al-Rusul wa'l Muluk*. It begins with an account of creation, the book traces the journey of humanity through the lives and careers of all the prominent Prophets including the final Messenger of Allah, Muhammad, his four rightly- guided Caliphs and the reign of the Umayyads before concluding with an entry in 915 CE. Although the original copy of this book was about sixty thousand pages long, the edition that has survived is much shorter. Even so, its English edition consists of forty bulky volumes, ten thousand pages in total.

Unlike al-Isfahani, al-Mas'udi (see chapter 44) or Ibn Khaldun (see chapter 75), al-Tabari was primarily a compiler of historical information. History, according to him, was no more than a sequence of events which he recorded and transmitted and did so without seeking to analyse or identify the underlying factors which triggered the sequence of events in the first place. That is why he meticulously recorded as much information as he could about the early Muslim community, without subjecting his data to rigorous examination or scrutiny. In that sense, he was very much like Herodotus, the ancient Greek historian, who also recorded his data without critically examining them.

For this reason, all prominent Islamic scholars, Qur'anic commentators and historians have continued to approach al-Tabari's history of the world with care and due diligence. But, given the size of the work, he probably thought it would be a hopeless task seeking to establish the authenticity of all the information he had collected, and thus left the task of sifting the wheat from the chaff to his successors such as al-Mas'udi, ibn al-Miskawayh and Ibn al-Athir.

After a lifetime devoted to the pursuit of Islamic sciences and history, al-Tabari, the 'father of Islamic history', passed away at the ripe old age of around eighty. But his remarkable contribution, especially in the field of *tafsir* and Islamic history, has remained unrivalled to this day.

39

Abu Bakr al-Razi
(b.854 - d.925 CE) / (b.226 - d.313 AH)

A visitor to the Chapel of Princeton University in the United States of America will notice the picture of a bearded, turban-wearing, Eastern-looking person represented on its window. According to George A. L. Sarton (b. 1884-d. 1856 CE), a renowned historian, the person shown on the window of the Chapel is 'the greatest clinician of Islam and the whole Middle Ages. He was the most celebrated and probably the most original of the Arabic writers.' This great Muslim physician and philosopher had such a great impact on medieval Christianity that the Christians considered it appropriate to mount his image inside a Chapel, their most sacred place of worship.

Although, during the medieval period, the Islamic world produced some of history's most influential philosophers, mathematicians and physicians, including Jabir ibn Hayyan (Geber), al-Kindi (Alkindus), al-Khwarizmi (Algorithm), Ibn Sina (Avicenna) and Ibn Rushd (Averroes), the Western world had not paid such a unique and glowing tribute to any other great Muslim thinker and scientist. Some historians have compared him with Hippocrates, the famous Greek physician. According to others, he was one of history's most innovative medical practitioners. This remarkable Muslim physician and philosopher was Abu Bakr al-Razi.

Muhammad ibn Zakariya ibn Yahya al-Razi, known in the West as Rhazes, was born in the Persian city of Rayy (close to modern Tehran, Iran), which was at the time a thriving centre of educational and commercial activity. Al-Razi was brought up and educated in Arabic, Persian and Islamic sciences. He then pursued advanced training in physical sciences with prominent local scholars like Ali ibn Sahl Rabban. As a brilliant student of Hunayn ibn Ishaq, who was a leading figure at the famous *Bait al-Hikmah* (The House of Wisdom) in Baghdad and translator of a large corpus of Greek philosophical and scientific works into Arabic. Rabban was widely recognised as a distinguished specialist in the physical sciences. Al-Razi thus studied physical sciences and aspects of philosophy under his guidance.

Thereafter, he became fascinated by music and musical theory, and during this period learned to play the flute with considerable proficiency. Then, while he was still in his late twenties, he became interested in alchemy and went on to rapidly master this subject, too. Inspired by the works of Jabir ibn Hayyan (see chapter 27), the father of Islamic chemistry, al-Razi became a widely respected authority on experimental alchemy. Unlike Jabir, however, he was more interested in the external or experimental part of alchemy, rather than the inner, mysterious or symbolic meaning of things and experiences.

When the passion of his chemical experimentation began to strain his eyesight, he was forced to reduce his chemical research and exploration. The continued weakening of his eyesight forced him to leave alchemy and chemistry for good. He then began to study medicine under Rabban's guidance.

As an eminent specialist in Greek, Syriac and Indian philosophy and medicine, Rabban taught him all parts of medicine until he acquired expertise in this subject, and also became thoroughly familiar with Greek philosophy. Being a gifted student and a wide-ranging reader, al-Razi soon became a respected intellectual and skilled medical practitioner. Although he started studying medicine in his late twenties, his single-minded dedication to his studies enabled him to master this subject within a short period. Indeed, he attained such proficiency in medicine that his reputation as a medical practitioner soon spread in and around Rayy. This prompted al-Mansur ibn Ishaq, the city's governor, to appoint him director of the local hospital.

As a physician and medical administrator, al-Razi was required to treat the sick and injured and to manage and coordinate the activities of the entire hospital. But in his spare time, he continued to read extensively and write productively on the philosophical and scientific thoughts of the day. In addition to mastering alchemy, medicine and philosophy, he acquired considerable proficiency in logic, cosmology, theology and mathematics. Indeed, al-Razi became an outstanding encyclopaedist who was familiar with all the major branches of learning known during his time. However, his contribution to the field of philosophy was quite considerable, both in terms of scope and quantity.

The majority of his philosophical works are no longer accessible. The small numbers which have survived provide abundant evidence of his mastery of Greek and Islamic philosophical thought. As a radical thinker, he helped to transform alchemy into a purely physical science by stripping it of its spiritual content (thus paving the way for the emergence of modern chemistry). He also adopted an equally radical approach to the study of philosophy. Unlike al-Ash'ari (see chapter 42) and al-Kindi (see chapter 35), he promoted a purely rationalistic philosophy. Thus, reason and revelation, he argued, were incompatible and any attempts to reconcile the two were bound to fail.

According to al-Razi, philosophy and religion cannot be reconciled because most religions, if not all, are opposed to philosophical rationalism and free scientific inquiry and research. Despite being thoroughly familiar with the philosophical ideas and thoughts of all the great ancient Greek thinkers like Pythagoras, Socrates, Plato, Democritus, Plotinus, Proclus and others, he became a champion of Platonic philosophy. Not surprisingly, his philosophical worldview focussed upon the five eternal principles of Creator, Universal Soul, Primeval Matter, Time and Space. But his critics such as Fakhr al-Din al-Razi (see chapter 63) and al-Shahrastani (b. 1086-d. 1158) accused him of being heavily influenced by non-Islamic ideas and thoughts, especially Manichaeism.

As such, these scholars dismissed his rationalistic interpretation of fundamental Islamic beliefs and practices as being heretical and unacceptable. There is no doubt that al-Razi's philosophical thought was influenced by a combination of Platonic and Manichaeistic ideas, which prompted him to promote a purely rationalistic approach to religion and thus reject the need for prophethood. Human reason, in his opinion, was far superior to revelation. That is why, he was one of the most rationalistic of all Muslim philosophers. Like the Mughal Emperor Akbar, he was a freethinker, but his philosophical thought never took off in the Muslim world. Certain aspects of al-Razi's philosophy were indeed misguided and heretical. However, it would be equally wrong to dismiss all of his philosophical material as being heretical, as that was not the case.

His philosophical excess aside, al-Razi led a thoroughly Islamic lifestyle. In his *Kitab al-Sirat al-Falsafiyah* (The Book of the Philosophical Way of Life), he explained how he had tried to lead a balanced and active life as a medical doctor, treating both the rich and poor to restore their health. He did so with Allah's help and support. Although accused of heresy, al-Razi's constant faith in Allah prevented his most vocal critics from branding him an unbeliever or atheist. Despite being financially very well-off, he shunned luxurious living and material extravagance. He rarely argued or quarrelled with anyone and was known to have been very fair and just in his dealings with others.

Indeed, he was in the habit of helping others, often at the expense of his own comfort and convenience. He led a simple, austere and disciplined lifestyle, thus avoiding excess in all matters except in the pursuit of knowledge and wisdom. He read extensively and wrote abundantly. On one occasion he wrote more than twenty thousand pages in a single year. And whenever he was informed that a learned scholar was visiting his locality, he used to go and sit in his company to learn something new. In old age, when he could no longer read or write due to failing eyesight, he paid people to read books to him so that he could continue to learn. In short, al-Razi's devotion and dedication to learning and scholarship was nothing short of remarkable.

If his philosophical thought was radical, then his contribution to medicine was truly remarkable. Along with Ibn Sina (see chapter 52) and al-Zahrawi (see chapter 46), he must be considered one of the most influential Muslim physicians of all time. Indeed, as a medical clinician, he was far superior to Ibn Sina because his diagnostic and observational skills were second to none. In addition to this, he was a supremely successful medical administrator who managed two of the leading hospitals of his day. One in Rayy and the other in Baghdad. When he was not in the hospitals, he taught and wrote regularly on all aspects of medicine. Thanks to his vast learning, advanced scientific methodology and clinical approach to medicine, students flocked to his house to learn from him. This forced him to turn one of his rooms into a study-cum-classroom, where he delivered regular lectures on all aspects of medicine, including how to recognise different illnesses, their symptoms and ways to treat them.

Being a cultured and dignified teacher, he used to treat all his students well and regularly provided free food to them. Later in life, he wrote a powerful critique of Greek medicine, especially Galen's cosmological and medical thought, under the title of 'Doubts about Galen'. In this book, he highlighted all the major errors contained in Galen's medical works. Al-Razi's other major medical contributions included, 'The Book of Mansur' and 'The Great Medical Book'.

'The Book of Mansur' was dedicated to his benefactor al-Mansur `ibn Ishaq, the Samanid governor of Rayy. It was an enormous encyclopaedia which provided a detailed exposition of all the major medical topics. This book was translated into Latin in the twelfth century by Gerard of Cremona and was used as a standard textbook on medicine across Europe until the sixteenth century. Likewise, his *Kitab al-Jami al-Kabir* (The Great Medical Book) was a voluminous encyclopaedia on medicine which not only covered all aspects of medicine in detail but also provided fresh clinical insights into the causes of different diseases and illnesses, as well as ways to treat them.

However, al-Razi's *Kitab al-Hawi fi al-Tibb* (The Comprehensive Book of Medicine), which was later translated into Latin, was arguably the most comprehensive medical work ever produced in Arabic. Consisting of twenty-five large volumes, this monumental work was much larger than Ibn Sina's famous The Canon of Medicine. It was his private medical notebook. He arranged it anatomically into thirty-seven different chapters. He provided a detailed explanation of all important medical topics including pathology, dermatology, personal hygiene, therapeutic techniques and other remedies he had learned from Greek, Indian, Babylonian and Syriac medicine. This book established his reputation as one of the most influential Muslim physicians and clinicians of all time.

His other famous works included, 'The Treatise on Smallpox and Measles'. As one of the oldest and most original treatises on smallpox and measles ever written, in this book, al-Razi accurately described these two deadly infections for the very first time. Originally translated into Latin in 1493, it was later published in French in 1762 and English in 1848 CE. It was considered to be one of the masterpieces of medical writing and used as a standard textbook on smallpox and measles until the modern period. In addition to this, al-Razi wrote extensively on gallstones, kidney, bladder and urinary diseases entitled, 'The Treatise on Stones in the Kidney and Bladder'.

According to Al-Biruni (see chapter 50), the famous Muslim scientist and historian, al-Razi authored one hundred and eighty-four books on all branches of learning, including eighty books on philosophical and theological topics alone. According to other historians, he wrote more than two hundred and forty books, most of which have, unfortunately, perished. More of his medical works have survived than his philosophical ones, perhaps because his approach to philosophy and theology was considered to be controversial.

By contrast, his medical works remained very influential both in the East and the West up to the modern day. He is hailed as the 'Arab Galen' across medieval Europe. Al-Razi became blind towards the end of his life, due to excessive reading and writing. He died at the age of about seventy-one and was buried in his native Rayy.

40

Al-Hallaj
(b.858 - d.922 CE) / (b.244 - d.310 AH)

The origin of Sufism (the spiritual part of Islam) is often linked to the Qur'an and the normal *Sunnah* (practice) of the Prophet by its followers. They argue that the sacred scriptures of Islam and its Prophet provide a genuine role model for those who seek to take the Islamic spiritual path. Therefore, far from being an alien interference in the Muslim world, Sufism represents the very heart and soul of Islam as a religion and way of life. The Prophet and his close *Sahabah* (companions like Abu Bakr, Umar, Uthman and Ali) were, according to the Sufis, the initiators and first exemplifiers of Islamic spirituality in its highest form. Like the Prophet and his close sahabah, the early Sufis, like Hasan al-Basri (see chapter 15), Ja'far al-Sadiq (see chapter 22) and Rabi'a al-Adawiyah (see chapter 25) surrendered worldly pleasures and engaged in worship and devotional activities and did so without using the label of Sufi.

However, when the Islamic region began to expand rapidly during the second half of the seventh century and the Muslims came into contact with the wealth and treasures of Persia and Byzantium for the first time, both the public and the ruling leaders began to submit to the temptations of uncontrolled wealth, luxury and materialism, which grew to threaten the foundation of early Islamic societies. At this critical time in Islamic history, many outstanding

Sufi personalities like Dawud al-Ta'i (d. 777 CE), Shaqiq al-Balkhi (d. 810 CE), Ibrahim ibn Adham (d. 782 CE), Maruf al-Karkhi (d. 815 CE), Hasan al-Basri and Rabi'a al-Adawiyah emerged to warn both the rulers and the people of the dangers of excessive materialism.

Although these personalities of Islam promoted a form of spirituality which was traditional in its content and outlook, later on, another group of influential Sufis would emerge to champion a more sophisticated and controversial form of Islamic spirituality. Al-Hallaj was probably one of the most well-known promoters of this type of Sufism.

Husayn ibn Mansur al-Hallaj was born at Tur in the Persian area of Fars. According to one report, his ancestors were originally Zoroastrians (followers of Zoroaster, the ancient Persian sage), while according to another source, he was a descendant of Abu Ayyub al-Ansari (b. 576-d. 674), who was a respected *Sahabi* of the Prophet. It is most likely that he had a Zoroastrian background and therefore did not have any family connection to Abu Ayyub al-Ansari. Either way, his father, Mansur, was a religious and devout Muslim who earned his living as a wool-carder; hence the title 'al-Hallaj'.

Young al-Hallaj committed the entire Qur'an to memory as a child as encouraged by his father. He then pursued further education in Arabic and traditional Islamic sciences. Thereafter, he travelled to the Iraqi city of Wasit where he completed his higher education under the guidance of its leading scholars. Wasit was founded in 702 CE by al-Hajjaj ibn Yusuf, the governor of the Umayyad ruler Abd al-Malik ibn Marwan (see chapter 16). It became a prominent centre of Islamic learning and scholarship in Iraq. Some of al-Hallaj's early teachers included Sahl al-Tustari (b. 818-d. 896 CE), one of the first to create the Sufi theory of *nur muhammadiya* (the Muhammadan Light); and author of a spiritual commentary on the Qur'an,; Abu Talib al-Makki (d. 996 CE);, the famous author of *Qut al-Qulub* (The Nourishment of Hearts), and al-Shibli (b. 861-d. 945 CE), who was also an influential Sufi scholar and theorist.

After completing his higher education, al-Hallaj left Wasit and moved to Basrah, which was also the home of Hasan al-Basri and Rabi'a al-Adawiyah, and there he married the daughter of a local Sufi. As an outspoken promoter of Islamic spiritual thought, he soon fell out with the local Sufis (including his father-in-law who accused him of being careless and insensitive). From Basrah, he went to Makkah where he became well-known for his devotional and ascetic practices. After completing the sacred *hajj*, he went to Baghdad which at the time was one of the Muslim world's foremost centres of Islamic learning and spirituality. Here he became a student of al-Junayd al-Baghdadi (b. 830-d. 910 CE), who was a Sufi scholar of great influence, and he personally taught him aspects of Islamic spiritual philosophy, but al-Hallaj soon fell out with him, too.

The story goes that one day he came and knocked on al-Junayd's door. When he asked who it was, al-Hallaj offensively replied, *'ana al-haqq'* ('I am the Truth', i.e., Allah). As a reserved Sufi, al-Junayd criticised him for his blasphemous and incorrect statement. When al-Hallaj refused to withdraw, al-Junayd broke his ties with him. Thereupon al-Hallaj left Baghdad and became a wandering Sufi. During his travels in and around Khurasan, he gathered around him a sizeable following and eventually went to Makkah to perform his second pilgrimage. From Makkah he went to Turkistan and from there he reportedly travelled to India and as far as the borders of China.

During his journeys, he developed and passionately spread his mystical ideas and thoughts. According to his critics, during his stay in India, he learnt the art of magic and, like al-Bistami (b. 804-d. 874 CE), became familiar with the Hindu mystical concepts of 'self-annihilation' and 'extinction' which, in turn, influenced his mystical views. He returned to Baghdad when he was about fifty and a large following gathered around him. But his extravagant mystical claims and utterances soon began to alarm and offend both the reserved Sufis and the orthodox religious scholars. He became such an outspoken supporter of Sufism that even the Mu'tazilites considered him to be an opportunist and fraud.

His outrageous spiritual claims not only stirred up a huge religious disagreement in Baghdad but also led to him being accused of supporting and sympathising with rebel political groups like the Qarmatians. This prompted the ruling Abbasid elites to expel him from Baghdad, after which he again returned to Makkah and performed yet another pilgrimage. After completing this third pilgrimage, he returned to Baghdad completely transformed. According to his son, Ahmad, during this period he claimed to have experienced the highest form of spiritual union where the distinction between 'I' and 'Thou' is removed, thus the lover and the object of his love become one (this is known as *ayn al-jam*).

While prominent Sufis like al-Junayd al-Baghdadi only communicated their mystical ideas and thoughts through *isharat* (hints or indications) to avoid offending both the religious scholars and the ruling elites, al-Hallaj ignored the advice of his fellow Sufis and began to promote the need for spiritual and moral reformation in the city of Baghdad. Though his call for moral and spiritual reformation was a powerful and important one as the forces of materialism and pleasure-seeking life began to become uncontrolled within the Muslim world, his unpredictable political outbursts and inflammatory mystical utterances offended everyone, including the Shi'a and the Mu'tazilites. He was eventually arrested by the Abbasid authorities and imprisoned for nine years.

During his imprisonment, he was at first treated well on account of his friendship with both the Abbasid vizier, Nasr al-Qashuri, and the mother of young Caliph al-Muqtadir (b. 895-d. 932 CE). But when the religious and political controversy he had generated showed no signs of decreasing, the Abbasid elites promptly put him on trial charged with blasphemy and treason. The trial was no more than a show; thus, everyone expected him to be found guilty. Mocked, criticised and branded a heretic (disbeleiver) by the orthodox religious scholars, and also shunned and expelled by his fellow Sufis, al-Hajjaj was sentenced to death. Were his mystical ideas and thoughts as objectionable and unorthodox as his opponents made them out to be? Did he deserve to be executed? Was he a religious maverick, as his detractors claimed, or was he a victim of religious intolerance and political persecution, as his supporters argued?

As one of the Muslim world's most radical and controversial mystical thinkers, al-Hallaj's life and thoughts are riddled with contradictions, paradoxes and unusual insights into Islamic spirituality. Following in the footsteps of al-Bistami (who was one of the first Sufi thinkers to argue that 'self-annihilation and extinction' represented the peak of spiritual experience), al-Hallaj became one of the most eloquent and bravest revealers of mystical secrets and truths. Indeed, he not only openly disclosed the secrets of Sufism to the public but went further and expressed his mystical feelings and experiences in a way that even the untrained could understand.

Central to al-Hallaj's mystical philosophy was the concept of *mahabbah* (love). Like Rabi'a al-Adawiyah, he encouraged the pursuit of disinterested love, that is to seek the Beloved (Allah) only for His sake, rather than out of fear of eternal ruin or promise of reward.

However, unlike Hasan al-Basri, Rabi'a al-Adawiyah and al-Junayd al-Baghdadi, all of whom unmistakably declared the traditional Islamic understanding of Divine Transcendence and Unity, al-Hallaj's expression of spontaneous, disinterested love proved hugely controversial because he claimed to have experienced *ayn al-jam* (the essence of union), where the lover and the Beloved (Allah) became one (a process called *ittihad*). Thus, he blurred the crucial distinction between Al-*Khaliq* (the creator) and *makhluq* (his creation). He expressed his mystical ideas and experiences in beautiful and refreshing poetic couplets. According to al-Nadim (b. 932-d. 995 CE), the famous bibliographer, al-Hallaj composed around forty-six books and essays on different topics of Islamic mysticism. However, his most famous works were his *Diwan* (collection of mystical odes) and *Kitab al-Tawasin* (The Book of Ta and Sin). The following quotations taken from these two books beautifully summarise the main thrust of his spiritual thought:

> 'I do not cease swimming in the seas of love, rising with the wave, then descending; now the wave sustains me, and then I sink beneath it; love bears me away where there is no longer any shore.' (Diwan al-Hallaj). 'I have seen my Lord with the eye of my heart, and I said: 'Who are you?' He said: 'You.' (Diwan al-Hallaj).

Taken literally, these mystical utterances and outbursts are indeed heretical and blasphemous. Not surprisingly, Baghdad's religious scholars and the ruling elites were shocked and horrified by these statements. Charged with the claim of personal deification, al-Hallaj argued he was neither a heretic nor a blasphemer; rather he was a promoter of mystical experience in its highest form. Sentenced to death at the age of sixty-four for preaching 'heretical' ideas, he refused to protest even when his over-zealous persecutors dragged him to the floor like a sack of potatoes and severely tortured and flogged him. His body was then cremated, and his ashes scattered in the Tigris.

Indeed, according to Farid al-Din Attar (b. 1145-d. 1221 CE), his sympathetic biographer, al-Hallaj danced to his death with joy and happiness, murmuring the words, 'All that matters for blissful is that the Unique should reduce him to Unity.' While his critics (such as Abu Talib al-Makki, al-Junyad al-Baghdadi, Ibn Hazm al-Andalusi [see chapter 53], Ibn Taymiyyah [see chapter 72] and Ibn Khaldun [see chapter 75]) have argued that he was a heretic and blasphemer because he claimed self-deification. Other equally renowned Islamic scholars and Sufis, like al-Shibli, al-Ghazali (see chapter 56), al-Jilani (see chapter 57), Fakhr al-Din al-Razi (see chapter 63), Rumi (see chapter 69) and Sir Muhammad Iqbal (see chapter 96), have cleared him of the charge of self-deification and belief in monism, i.e., Allah and the creation are the same. As for Abdullah Ansari (b. 1006-d. 1088 CE) of Herat, in his *Tabaqat al-Sufiya* (Generations of Sufis), he chose to sit on the fence; neither approving of al-Hallaj nor rejecting him.

However, a closer study of his mystical ideas and thoughts shows that he was far from being a blasphemer or pantheist. This view has also been favoured, and proved quite conclusively, by the renowned French scholar and Islamicist, Louis Massignon (b. 1883-d. 1962 CE). In his work, 'The Passion of al-Hallaj, Mystic and Martyr of Islam', he argued that al-Hallaj adopted a form of *wahdat al-shuhud* (Unity of Witnesses) rather than *wahdat al-wujud* (Unity of Being). If this view is correct, then al-Hallaj was neither a heretic nor a religious maverick; instead, his unusual, spontaneous spiritual flashes and utterances were both misunderstood and misinterpreted by the Sufis as well as the religious scholars of his time.

By sending al-Hallaj to death, argued Massignon, the Abbasid elites not only wrongly satisfied the wishes of the religious authorities, but they also diverted attention away from the social, political and economic challenges and difficulties of the time and in so doing, they committed an injustice. True to form, nearly eleven centuries after his death, al-Hallaj continues to divide the Sufis, Islamic scholars, philosophers, jurists and theologians to this day.

41

Al-Farabi
(b.870 - d.950 CE) / (b.257 - d.339 AH)

Whilst ancient Greek philosophy and science, as championed by outstanding thinkers like Socrates, Plato and Aristotle was completely neglected in the West, the Muslims – in the Islamic East – embraced their ideas with open arms. The Muslim philosophers, scientists and translators not only preserved these philosophical and scientific contributions but also carried out an organised analysis and evaluation of ancient Greek thought. By doing this they made significant original contributions of their own.

Thanks largely to the tireless efforts of the early Muslim scientists and philosophers, today the thoughts of Plato, Aristotle, Galen and Hippocrates have become widely known both in the East and the West. As a matter of fact, the Western world came to discover ancient Greek philosophy and science as late as the fourteenth and fifteenth centuries, facilitated by the Muslims of *al-Andalus* (Islamic Spain). More than any other Islamic philosopher, al-Farabi acquired a thorough mastery of ancient Greek philosophy before he went on to develop an organised interpretation of *falsafah* (Islamic philosophy) for the very first time.

Muhammad ibn Muhammad al-Farabi is better known in the Latin West as Alpharabius. He was born in Wasij, a village located near Farab in the province of Transoxiana in Turkistan (Turkestan).

Of Turkish origin, his father initially served as an army captain, and later he became a prominent member of the Persian military service. Although his father wanted his son to follow in his footsteps and join the elite Persian army, destiny had other plans for the young al-Farabi. During his early years, he attended his local schools and followed the standard curriculum which included Arabic, Persian, poetry, literature and Islamic sciences, focusing primarily on the Qur'an and Prophetic traditions.

Since Farab and its surrounding areas came under Muslim rule only a few decades before al-Farabi's birth, his family may have embraced Islam during this period and become followers of the *Shafi'i* madhhab (a school of legal thought), which had spread throughout that region. This prompted young al-Farabi to specialise in *Shafi'i* jurisprudence. As a bright student, he excelled in his studies beyond his family's expectations and was encouraged to pursue higher education rather than follow his father's military career.

From an early age, he showed an interest in all the sciences of his day and acquired expertise in several languages and dialects. Blessed with a matchless language ability, he continued to develop this ability throughout his life and probably knew more languages and dialects than any other Muslim thinker of his generation. Arabic and Persian aside, he mastered Turkish, Greek, Syriac and Hebrew, not to mention many other local languages and dialects. Though short in stature, al-Farabi always dressed immaculately and was very fond of beautiful Turkish attire, even though he became most famous for his uncontrollable thirst for knowledge and wisdom.

He was brought up and educated at a time when the Samanid ruler Nasr ibn Ahmad (b. 906-d. 943 CE) actively promoted learning and higher education. Al-Farabi went on to receive advanced training in linguistics and Islamic sciences. He became so proficient in *fiqh* (Islamic jurisprudence) that he was appointed *qadi* (judge) while he was still in his twenties. He later became bored with legal and administrative work. As a natural-born thinker and philosopher, he found the dull nature of legal routine suffocating and abandoned his legal career in favour of higher education in the philosophical sciences.

After studying philosophy under the guidance of famous local scholars, he began to travel in search of further knowledge. From Farab, he moved to Merv (in present-day Turkmenistan), which was a prominent centre of religious and philosophical learning and where some of the leading scholars of the day lived and taught. Here he studied logic and philosophy under the guidance of Yuhanna ibn Haylan, who was a master of philosophy and a leading practitioner of Greek thought. It was in Merv that he encountered Greek philosophy for the first time and began to study the major works of Aristotle in Greek, as well as in Syriac translation. So, he became one of the first Muslim philosophers to study Aristotelian logic and philosophy directly from the original Greek under the guidance of some of its leading authorities. As a result, he rapidly acquired ancient Greek philosophical thought.

From Merv, he went to Baghdad, which was the capital of the Abbasid Caliphate and one of the Muslim world's foremost centres of learning at the time. Al-Farabi arrived in Baghdad when he was around thirty. He pursued advanced training in Arabic grammar under the guidance of Abu Bakr ibn al-Sarraj, who was one of the most distinguished grammarians of his generation. He was impressed with al-Farabi's profound knowledge of logic. Al-Sarraj asked him to teach him logic. After several years in Baghdad, he travelled to the northern Iraqi city of Harran and from there he went to Constantinople (modern Istanbul) before finally returning to Baghdad.

Thus, at the age of forty, al-Farabi became widely recognised as a prominent jurist, logician, philosopher, linguist and theologian. Given his remarkable academic achievements, he could have started teaching on his arrival in Baghdad, but instead joined the class of Matta ibn Yunus, who was one of the most respected Arabic translators of Aristotle's works. After completing his advanced training in Aristotelian logic under Matta's guidance, he became an unrivalled master of Greek philosophical sciences. He then became one of the foremost authorities on the thought of Aristotle, and also the first systematic Muslim philosopher.

Al-Farabi lived in Baghdad for another three decades, during which he taught and pursued research on all the sciences of his day. Given his prodigious learning and scholarship, he could have acquired much fame and wealth if he wished. Instead, he shunned public life, wealth and glamour in favour of a life devoted entirely to learning and teaching knowledge and wisdom. As a bookworm and an extensive reader, he reportedly read Aristotle's Physics more than forty times and his De Anima around two hundred times. He produced nearly seventy volumes of notes and writings on all parts of philosophy. And although this figure may be somewhat exaggerated, the fact that al-Farabi was a gifted scholar, and an industrious writer is not in doubt. As an outstanding walking encyclopedia, he was thoroughly familiar with all the branches of learning known during his time. He became most famous for his contributions to three disciplines: logic, political science, philosophy and metaphysics. His works on these subjects are considered to be nothing short of great monuments in the histories of human thought.

Al-Farabi's writings are unusually simple and easy to understand as they are without philosophical and technical jargon. Thus, even those who are not philosophically minded can read and make sense of his ideas and thoughts without much difficulty. Despite being familiar with more than twenty languages and dialects, he deliberately chose to write all his works in Arabic. This was perhaps because Arabic was the language of the Qur'an – the official language of Islamic learning and scholarship – and also the common language of the Muslim world at the time. Another reason could be that he wanted to reach a large audience, in which case Arabic again would have been his obvious choice.

Al-Farabi authored most of his books during his long stay in Baghdad, although some were composed during the final years of his life in Syria. In total, he wrote over a hundred books on all the sciences of his time including seventeen commentaries, fifteen essays and around sixty books and manuscripts. Sadly, the vast majority of his works have perished; only a small number – no more than twenty – have survived, primarily in Hebrew and Latin translations.

Of his major writings, the most important were *Kitab Ihsa al-Ulum* (The Book of Enumeration of Sciences) and 'The Commentary on Aristotle's Physics'. In addition to this, he wrote several treatises disproving the ideas of other prominent Muslim philosophers like Abu Bakr al-Razi. In his *Kitab Ihsa al-Ulum*, al-Farabi – for the first time in Islamic intellectual history – developed a coherent and comprehensive classification of the sciences of his day. In doing so, he – again for the very first time – analysed, interpreted and introduced Greek philosophical sciences into the Muslim world in a systematic way. His commentaries on the works of Aristotle were some of the most scholarly and wide-ranging books to have been produced on Aristotelian logic and philosophy.

This rightly earned him the popular title of *al-mu'allim al-thani* (The Second Teacher) with Aristotle being *al-mu'allim al-awwal* (The First Teacher). If al-Farabi was a great philosopher, then he was an equally matchless champion of logic. His contribution in this field was so vast and original that he became widely known as 'the father of logic'. So much so that the great Jewish philosopher and theologian Musa bin Maimon (b. 1138-d. 1204 CE), once told one of his friends that al-Farabi's works on logic were 'finer than flour' and urged him not to bother consulting the works of other logicians.

Unlike Imam al-Ghazali and many other prominent Islamic thinkers, al-Farabi considered philosophy to be entirely unified. He was also of the opinion that in essence there was only one true philosophy. Thus, he argued that both Plato and Aristotle explained the same truth. He communicated these views in his book, 'The Book of Reconciliation of the Opinions of the Two Divines, Plato and Aristotle'. After harmonising the philosophical thoughts of Plato and Aristotle, he argued that similar harmony existed between Islam and Greek philosophy. As an unlimited reader of Islamic scriptural sources and Greek thought, he devoted a considerable part of his intellectual life to seeking to reconcile these two supposedly conflicting worldviews.

Al-Ghazali questioned and attacked certain parts of al-Farabi's cosmology, and even accused him of blindly following Aristotle and other prominent Greek philosophers on issues such as the nature of creation and the theory of the intellect. However, al-Farabi's philosophical thinking also greatly influenced al-Ghazali himself and other famous Islamic philosophers.

As a devout Muslim and also a practising Sufi, al-Farabi focused more on the spiritual, than on the practical dimension of things. Nevertheless, he found time to think about and write abundantly on both political philosophy and ethics. Indeed, he was one of the first to write on these subjects in the Muslim world. In summary, his political philosophy and *ilm al-madani* (science of society) were underpinned by an integrated spiritualist view of human life and society. One where the achievement of current happiness and eternal salvation went hand in hand — as opposed to emphasising the importance of one without the other.

In other words, his approach to political philosophy and ethics was this-worldly and simultaneously other-worldly. That is to say, he combined the practical and spiritual dimensions of Islam to create a solid foundation for a balanced social, political and ethical framework. He developed his political and ethical ideas in many treatises including, 'The Book of Political Governance' and 'The Book of Attainment of Happiness'. Inspired by Islamic scriptural sources, as well as ancient Greek thinkers like Plato, Plotinus and Aristotle, he developed a refreshingly unified political synthesis in these books and took into consideration the practical and spiritual dimensions of human life and society. Also, the fact that he was an expert in traditional Islamic sciences, and specialised in *Shafi'i* jurisprudence, comes across more clearly in his political and ethical works than it does in his philosophical and cosmological output.

Al-Farabi was in his early seventies when political instability began to spread across Baghdad, and this prompted him to move to Damascus in 942 CE. Here he worked as a gardener for a period before moving to Egypt, only to return to Damascus again in 949 CE. This time he received a warm welcome from the reigning Hamanid ruler, Sayf al-Dawlah, who invited him to join his royal court. But a spiritually inclined al-Farabi politely refused the monarch's offer. The ruler then offered him a large sum of money. He refused that too, saying he only needed an allowance of four dirhams to cover his daily expenses so that he could continue his study and research. A year later, al-Farabi died at the age of eighty and was buried in Damascus following a simple funeral. Like al-Khwarizmi (see chapter 32), al-Kindi (see chapter 35) and Abu Bakr al-Razi (see chapter 39), he was a genius and one of the most influential Muslim philosophers of all time.

It is not surprising, therefore, that his ideas and thoughts influenced some of the most famous thinkers of the Muslim world including Ibn Sina (see chapter 52), al-Ghazali (see chapter 56), Ibn Tufayl (see chapter 58), Ibn Rushd (see chapter 60), Ibn Khaldun (see chapter 75) and Shah Waliullah (see chapter 86). Likewise, his works influenced prominent Jewish and Christian thinkers like St. Thomas Aquinas, John Duns Scotus, Musa bin Maimon (Maimonides) and Leo Strauss among others.

42

Abul Hasan al-Ash'ari
(b.873 - d.941 CE) / (b.260 - d.328 AH)

After the death of Caliph Uthman in June 656 CE, a huge controversy arose within the Islamic region about the question of leadership and political authority. During this period, several political factions emerged. These included the *shi'at Ali, khawarij, murji'ah* and the *mu'tazilah*. These groups emerged due to differences of opinion over political matters. Later, they developed their own distinct philosophical and theological views. Of these sects, the most politically neutral were the *mu'tazilah* who later acquired a largely philosophical and theological form under the influence of Wasil ibn 'Ata. He was a student of Hasan al-Basri (see chapter 15) but parted company (*i'tizal*) with his tutor following a bitter dispute between the two men.

Under Wasil's guidance, Mu'tazilism became an influential philosophical and theological network. Wasil was heavily influenced by political Mu'tazilism and Greek philosophical thought, so he and his friends developed a distinct Mu'tazilite creed. This was based on using reason to understand and interpret the nature of Allah, *dhat wa sifat Allah* (his essence and attributes), *kalam Allah* (the concept of divine speeh) and the purpose of creation. The Mu'tazilite philosophical explanations of these Islamic beliefs were opposed by the traditionalists. But it received a favourable reception from the Abbasid rulers. Thus, famous Abbasid rulers like Harun al-Rashid (see chapter 28) and his son al-Ma'mun (see chapter 33) became strong champions of Mu'tazilism. In fact, under al-Ma'mun's rule, this creed was declared the dominant theology of the State. At a time when orthodoxy (the generally accepted beliefs) was avoided and heterodoxy (departing from the tradition) became common, Abul Hasan al-Ash'ari, one of the Muslim world's *mutakallimun* (most influential theologians), emerged to turn the tables on Mu'tazilism.

Abul Hasan Ali ibn Isma'il al-Ash'ari was also known as *Imam al-Mutakallimun* (chief of the theologians) and *Imam Ahl al-Sunnah wa'l Jama'ah* (chief of the mainstream Sunni Muslims). He was born in Basrah, in modern Iraq into a distinguished Muslim family which traced its lineage back to Abu Musa al-Ash'ari, who was a famous *Sahabi* (companion) of the Prophet. His father, Isma'il, was a learned and highly respected citizen of Basrah. He died when al-Ash'ari was still a youngster, and this forced his family into poverty. Young al-Ash'ari thus suffered considerable personal hardship until his mother married Abu Ali Muhammad al-Jubba'i, who was one of the grand students of Wasil ibn Ata. Al-Jubba'i was based at the Mu'tazilite Basrah headquarters where he was widely respected as one of the great promoters of Mu'tazilism. Al-Ash'ari was now being brought up and educated under the guidance and care of a leading figure of philosophical rationalism and freethinking. He also mastered Arabic grammar, literature, Islamic sciences and the philosophical and theological principles of Mu'tazilism from an early age.

As a teacher and writer, al-Jubba'i was a powerful champion of Mu'tazilism, but he was not known for his debating or public speaking skills. As al-Ash'ari was raised and nurtured in the home of Mu'tazilism, he became a committed and expert interpreter of Mu'tazilite beliefs and doctrines. He mastered philosophical rationalism sufficiently so that he could discuss the finer points of Mu'tazilite philosophy when he was barely twenty years old. His vast knowledge and debating skills soon earned him much fame and approval, even during al-Jubbai's lifetime. Thus, everyone expected al-Ash'ari to follow in the footsteps of his aged teacher, mentor and stepfather. He was expected to become a champion of Mu'tazilism after al-Jubba'i's death.

When al-Jubba'i died in Basrah, al-Ash'ari was forty-two. By this time he was already widely recognised as one of the most learned Mu'tazilite theologians of his generation. Although there were other respected Mu'tazilite scholars around at the time (including Abul Hashim, the son of al-Jubba'i, and others) Imam al-Ash'ari was far superior to all of them because he had mastered the finer points of Mu'tazilite philosophy and theology. Furthermore, in comparison to the other Mu'tazilite thinkers of the time, he was a better debater especially when it came to defending Mu'tazilism against its traditionalist rivals. In short, al-Ash'ari was in a league of his own. So following Abu Ali al-Jubba'i's death, he became the undisputed leader and champion of this philosophical creed. Now everyone expected al-Ash'ari to succeed al-Jubba'i as the outstanding leader of Mu'tazilism. But events took an unexpected turn. According to al-Ash'ari, the Prophet Muhammad appeared to him in a dream and instructed him to champion the cause of Islamic orthodoxy, rather than that of Mu'tazilism. This Prophetic intervention proved decisive as far as al-Ash'ari was concerned. Although he considered himself to be a defender of the Mu'tazilite creed, the Prophet's rejection of Mu'tazilite beliefs and practices shook al-Ash'ari to his core. He thus confined himself to his house for about two weeks. He went through a period of intense soul-searching and coming to terms with his new experience.

After nearly forty years of learning, refining, mastering and hair-splitting debates and discussions on the finer points of Mu'tazilite philosophy and theology, it all now appeared to him to be false. Otherwise, why would the Prophet of Allah appear to him in a dream and show him the way forward? Suddenly, it was as if al-Ash'ari woke up from a deep sleep and discovered that he had spent four decades of his life studying and championing the cause of an un-Islamic belief system. According to al-Ash'ari, the unexpected visitation from the Prophet, coupled with the Divine *nur* (light) and *barakah* (blessing) which was bestowed on him, enabled him to overcome his dilemma. After fifteen days of deep reflection, intense self-examination and intellectual repositioning, he emerged from his house on a Friday afternoon before *salat al-jumu'ah*. He went straight to the central mosque in Basrah, which at the time was packed to its maximum capacity. He stepped onto the *minbar* (pulpit) and delivered a historic announcement. This announcement was to mark the beginning of the end of philosophical rationalism and the revival of Islamic traditionalism.

In his unique and matchless style, al-Ash'ari proclaimed: 'He who knows me, knows who I am. He who does not know me, let him know that I am Abul Hasan Ali al-Ash'ari. I used to believe that the Qur'an was created. I used to believe that the eyes of men shall not see Allah and that the creatures create their actions. Lo! I repent that I have been a Mu'tazilite. I reject these opinions. I take the opportunity to disprove the Mu'tazilites and expose their inconsistencies and wickedness.'

His public rejection of Mu'tazilism represented a milestone in Islamic intellectual history as the battleline between Islamic orthodoxy and philosophical rationalism now became clear because the Mu'tazilite rationalists had lost one of their most formidable champions. Before his conversion to Islamic orthodoxy, the Mu'tazilites dealt with the traditionalists' attacks on their beliefs with ease. But following his conversion, al-Ash'ari now became their intellectual troublemaker par excellence. The Mu'tazilites found themselves caught between a rock and a hard place.

As expected, a new Imam al-Ash'ari then launched a systematic and full-blown attack on the philosophical and theological foundations of their creed. Having studied Mu'tazilite ideas under the guidance of its best thinkers (Abu Ali al-Jubba'i) and mastered the art of philosophical and theological discussion, he now became the most difficult intellectual challenger for the Mu'tazilites. They were unable to answer his consistent and stinging philosophical and theological attacks on the foundations of their school of thought. The Mu'tazilites suddenly found themselves stranded in an intellectual no-man's land.

Al-Ash'ari's withdrawal from Mu'tazilism was both comprehensive and extremely effective. He composed more than ninety books on *aqida* (all aspects of Isdlamic beliefs) and *kalam* (theology), to reject the Mu'tazilite creed and parts of Islamic philosophy. In so doing, he developed a powerful combination of *aql* (reason) and *wahy* (revelation). He reconciled philosophical rationalism, Islamic beliefs and religious statements. One of his most famous books is *Maqalat al-Islamiyin* (Beliefs of Muslims).

In his books, he provided a systematic explanation of the core Islamic theological beliefs. These were based on his excellent knowledge of the original Islamic sources and his thorough familiarity with the methods of the philosophers. Imam Al-Ash'ari was rated very highly by the scholars of Islam, so much so that Ibn Taymiyyah (see chapter 72) wrote that he had not come across another book like the *Maqalat*.

As philosophical rationalists, the Mu'tazilites believed in the superiority of the human mind. That means, they considered *wahy* (Divine revelation) to be a servant to *aql* (human reason). Not surprisingly, they interpreted fundamental Islamic concepts – *tawhid* (the oneness of Allah), *al-asma wa'l sifat* (Divine Names and Attributes), and the nature of the Qur'an – from a purely rationalistic perspective. The traditionalists considered such an interpretation of Islam to be unorthodox and blameworthy. They also considered the Mu'tazilites to be heretics and innovators in religious matters.

The traditionalists were led by eminent Islamic scholars like Imam Ahmad ibn Hanbal (see chapter 31). They intensely opposed the philosophical interpretation of Islamic theological matters. They considered *zahiri* (the external) meaning of the Divine revelation (the Qur'an) and the *Hadith* (Prophetic traditions) to be sufficient for human guidance. By contrast, al-Ash'ari considered both of these views to be wrong and extreme. Instead, he took the middle path. He argued that revelation and reason were equally necessary for creating a balanced interpretation and understanding of Islamic thought and worldview. He therefore devoted all his time and energy to reconciling these two extreme views, which at the time competed for the hearts and minds of the Muslims.

Al-Ash'ari refuted the Mu'tazilite belief that Divine Attributes were not real and that human beings would not be able to see Allah in the hereafter without Him having to reincarnate Himself in a non-human form. In response, Al-Ash'ari stated that the Qur'an was *ghair makhluq* (the created), eternal Word of Allah and that only the ink, paper and individual letters were created. Unlike the Mu'tazilites, he further clarified that the Prophet Muhammad could intercede on behalf of Muslims in the next life, if he wished, by Allah's permission. This way, one by one, Imam al-Ash'ari demolished the heretical beliefs of the rationalists and reestablished traditional Islamic positions on all important theological matters.

Imam al-Ash'ari emerged at a time when Mu'tazilism was already on the decline following the death of Caliphs Mu'tasim Bi'llah and al-Wathiq Bi'llah. Along with Abdullah al-Ma'mun (see chapter 33), these two Abbasid rulers became very powerful supporters of the Mu'tazilite creed. But this situation changed immediately after another Caliph Mutawakkil 'ala Allah ascended the Abbasid throne. He demoted all the supporters of Mu'tazilism from the highest ranks of power. He also replaced traditional Islam as the official religion of the Abbasid Empire. Despite this, the intellectual legacy of Wasil ibn Ata and his Mu'tazilite creed continued within the intellectual and cultural circles of the Abbasid Empire. But thanks to al-Ash'ari's sustained and merciless critique of philosophical rationalism, the Mu'tazilite creed was eventually rooted out from the intellectual and cultural lives of Muslims.

Imam al-Ash'ari was not only an outstanding Islamic intellectual; he was also one of the greatest religious thinkers of all time. Not surprisingly, his religious thought and intellectual legacy continue to exert a profound influence on the way Muslims think, behave and lead their lives to this day. He died and was buried in a place close to *Bab al-Basrah* (the Gate of Basrah). He was sixty-eight at the time.

After his death, some of his prominent successors such as Imam Abu Ja'far al-Tahawi of Egypt and Imam Abu Mansur al-Maturidi of Muslim Central Asia presented a *kalam* (unified theology), which they hoped would be acceptable to Muslims of all backgrounds. From that day on, Ash'arism became the most dominant religious theology in the Muslim world.

43

Abd al-Rahman III
(b.890 - d.961 CE) / (b.277 - d.350 AH)

The Umayyads ruled the Muslim world from 661 to 750 CE, but when the Abbasids took over they put most of the Umayyad princes to the sword. Only a handful of Umayyad princes escaped the massacre. Abd al-Rahman I (see chapter 26), the grandson of Umayyad ruler Hisham, was one of them. He fled Damascus and travelled on foot and by ship for many years before he finally reached North Africa, where he received a warm welcome from the Berber tribe of Banu Nafisa (in present-day Morocco). During his stay there he received news of the political chaos which prevailed across the sea in *al-Andalus* (Islamic Spain) at the time. He was informed that the Muslims in Spain had become bitterly divided. One faction supported the present governor, Yusuf al-Fihri, while the other group opposed him. Prince Abd al-Rahman immediately contacted the governor's opponents and requested their help to overthrow him.

He then led an army into battle and defeated the governor's forces before proceeding to Cordova, the capital of *al-Andalus*. In doing so, Abd al-Rahman I began Umayyad rule in Spain. He was also known as *al-Dhakil* (the Immigrant) and *sahib al-Andalus* (the Master of Islamic Spain) because of his outstanding political leadership and organisational ability. Abd al-Rahman I and his descendants went on to rule Muslim Spain for nearly three centuries. During this period, Muslim Spain produced several influential rulers, but the most outstanding of them all was Caliph Abd al-Rahman III.

Abd al-Rahman ibn Muhammad, better known as Abd al-Rahman III, was born in Cordova during the reign of his grandfather, Amir Abdullah ibn Muhammad (b. 844-d. 912 CE). When Abd al-Rahman was still a boy, his father was poisoned by one of his uncles due to political in-fighting. Young Abd al-Rahman therefore grew up under the care of his Frankish mother, Muzna, and his grandfather, Amir Abdullah. As a youngster, he received a varied education including tutorials on the Qur'an, Islamic moral and ethical teachings, as well as Arabic literature, poetry and history. He was short in height, of muscular build and had dark blue eyes and somewhat reddish hair, making his appearance more European than Arab.

Although his grandfather Abdullah ruled Islamic Spain from 888 to 912 CE, he proved to be both incompetent and cruel. Unsurprisingly, political instability and civil disorder soon broke out across the land. His decision to use force rather than engage in dialogue with his opponents created political friction and mass dissatisfaction against his rule. It also undermined the current situation and alienated his people. During his twenty-two-year reign, he failed to maintain the peace, wealth and progress achieved by his famous predecessors (such as Abd al-Rahman II and Muhammad I). Young Abd al-Rahman was aware of the difficult challenges which confronted his country and contributed as much as he could to improve the problems until Amir Abdullah died in 912 CE.

He succeeded his grandfather at the age of twenty-two and became the new ruler of Islamic Spain. By then he was already recognised as an experienced politician, having played a prominent role in the country's political and civil administration under his grandfather. However, unlike his grandfather, he became an able, wise and gifted ruler and politician. Widely respected and admired by his people, his accession to the throne brought much joy and happiness throughout the country. Being also a just, kind and compassionate ruler, his reign marked a fresh start for Islamic Spain.

Since Abd al-Rahman considered the post of Caliphate to be an enormous trust and responsibility which his people had placed on his young shoulders, he was determined not to let them down. Immediately after becoming Caliph, his main priority was to restore political stability and civil order across *al-Andalus*. He thus appealed to his people for their help, for without their co-operation, he told them, he would not be able to pull Islamic Spain back from the brink of civil war. He spelt out the choice facing his people honestly. The choice, he stated, was one of life or death, survival or extinction. Without political unity, social solidarity and religious harmony, the Muslims of Spain faced the serious danger of being destroyed by their Christian opponents who were closely monitoring the social and political situation in Islamic Spain at the time.

He reminded his people that the Abbasid Caliph in Baghdad would not come to their aid should the neighbouring Christian powers decide to attack *al-Andalus*. His message to his people was very loud and clear: unite or you will be dispatched to the dustbin of history. Moved by Abd al-Rahman's message of hope, reconciliation and unity, the bitterly divided Muslims of Spain finally laid down their arms and united under his wise and able leadership. Unlike his grandfather, Abd al-Rahman was a gifted communicator who preferred to talk and engage in dialogue with his opponents rather than use force. His honesty and friendly approach endeared him to his people so much that he managed to restore peace, order and stability across the country within the first three months of his reign.

After establishing political and civil order across Cordova and its immediate surroundings, Abd al-Rahman turned his attention to other major cities like Seville and Toledo, which at the time were ruled by various rebellious groups who had taken control of those cities in open disobedience of the central government. He was determined not to allow this state of affairs to continue. He sent delegations to the rulers of those cities to reassert his political authority over them. But when these self-appointed rulers rejected his peace-making measures, he launched military actions against them. His forces defeated their enemies and marched into Seville in 913 CE without encountering much resistance. However, Muhammad, the governor of Seville, allied himself with Abd al-Rahman and continued to serve as governor of that city. By contrast, Toledo presented a different offer altogether. When the ruler and people of the city fought Abd al-Rahman's forces, he laid siege to it, and it was nearly two years before the people of Toledo unconditionally surrendered to him.

During this period, Abd al-Rahman found himself fighting a battle on two fronts. On the one hand, he was busy fighting the rebellious Muslim rulers inside Islamic Spain itself. On the other hand, he was forced to take action against the invading Christians of the north. They were encouraged by the chaos which existed within the Muslim territories at the time. So Abd al-Rahman decided to launch fresh raids against them. Since Ordono II, the Christian ruler of Leon, was the chief instigator of these raids, Abd al-Rahman sent an expedition and inflicted a crushing defeat on his forces. The overthrow of the Christians in the north brought much-needed peace and tranquillity in *al-Andalus*.

He then instigated military action against the constant mischief-maker, Umar ibn Hafsun, the ruler of Bobastro. Eventually, this territory was also brought under his rule. After successfully defeating these cities, Abd al-Rahman finally restored peace, order and security across much of *al-Andalus*. Thanks to his vision, courage and bravery, Abd al-Rahman won over the hearts and minds of his people. Thus, in 929 CE, at the age of thirty-nine, he became the undisputed master of Islamic Spain and adopted the title of *al-khalifah al-nasir li-din Allah* (the Caliph, the Defender of the Religion of Allah). This was to mark the beginning of a new era of political stability, economic prosperity and great scientific and cultural achievements across Muslim Spain under the outstanding leadership and patronage of Caliph Abd al-Rahman III.

Indeed, under his stewardship, Spain became a beacon of light for the rest of Europe. He built beautiful mosques, schools and colleges and promoted learning and education throughout *al-Andalus*. When there was hardly a college or library worth its name in Europe, *al-Andalus* boasted some of the finest, and also largest, libraries and educational institutions in the Western world. Subsequently, students flocked from the rest of Europe to Cordova, the magnificent capital of Islamic Spain, to study under the tutelage of some of Europe's most influential Muslim philosophers, scientists and intellectuals like Ibn Hazm (see chapter 53), Ibn Bajjah (Avempace), Ibn Tufayl (Abubacer, see chapter 58) and Ibn Rushd (Averroes, see chapter 60), who transformed the Academy in Cordova into one of the world's most dazzling centres of higher education and research.

Also, during Abd al-Rahman's glorious reign, Cordova reached its cultural height, boasting more than six-hundred elegant mosques, fifty hospitals, nine-hundred public baths and countless markets. The town centre was in turn surrounded by two-hundred-thousand beautiful houses. It was connected by well-planned roads and streets which were illuminated during the night by roadside lamps – and at a time when the rest of Europe was still lingering in the Dark Ages. The thriving and tolerant civil society, known as the *convivencia*, created by Caliph Abd al-Rahman enabled everyone including Muslims, Jews and Christians to live and work together in peace and tranquillity.

The Jews were granted full freedom to lead their lives according to the rules of their faith and culture. Indeed, under Islamic rule, the Jews and Judaism flourished in Spain to the extent that this period of Jewish history is widely considered to be the Golden Age of Judaism by the European Jews. Renowned Jewish scholars and thinkers such as Soloman ibn Gabirol and Judah Halevi also lived and thrived in Islamic Spain.

Then, in 936 CE, Caliph Abd al-Rahman ordered the construction of a new palace city which became known *as madinat al-zahra* (the dazzling city). This mammoth project took more than forty years to complete. It became known later as the 'tenth century Versailles'. The splendour and magnificence of *madinat al-zahra* was simply breathtaking. Considered to have been an architectural masterpiece, it remained an unrivalled architectural structure throughout Europe for a long time. Although Abd al-Rahman indeed started this project, unfortunately, he could not complete it. Caliph al-Hakam II (b. 915-d. 976 CE), his son and successor, completed it. As a passionate builder, Abd al-Rahman also constructed a large number of magnificent palaces, but nothing was to compare with his immortal *madinat al-zahra* in both size and beauty. It was not only a landmark in European cultural history; it was also a lasting tribute to the memory of one of Islamic Spain's most influential rulers.

In his book, The Muslims of Spain (1886 CE), the distinguished historian Stanley Lane-Poole summed up Islamic achievements in Spain in these words:

'For nearly eight centuries, under her Mohammedan rulers, Spain set to all Europe a shining example of a civilized and enlightened State. Her fertile provinces, rendered doubly prolific by the industry and engineering skill of her conquerors, bore fruit a hundredfold. Innumerable cities sprang up in the rich valleys of the Guadelquivir and the Guadiana, whose names, and names only, still commemorate the vanished glories of their past. Art, literature and science prospered, as they then prospered nowhere else in Europe. Students flocked from France, Germany and England to drink from the fountain of learning, which flowed only in the cities of the Moors. The surgeons and doctors of Andalusia were in the van of science: women were encouraged to devote themselves to serious study, and female doctors were not unknown among the people of Cordova. Mathematics, astronomy and botany, history, philosophy and jurisprudence were to be mastered in Spain and Spain alone. The practical work of the field, the scientific methods of irrigation, the arts of fortification and shipbuilding, the highest and most elaborate products of the loom, the graver and the hammer, the potter's wheel and the mason's trowel were all brought to perfection by the Spanish Moors. In the practice of war, no less than in the arts of peace, they long stood supreme. Their fleets disputed the command of the Mediterranean with the Fatimites while their armies carried fire and sword through the Christian marches. The Cid himself, the national hero, long fought on the Moorish side, and in all save education was more than half a Moor. Whatsoever makes a kingdom great and prosperous, whatsoever tends to refinement and civilisation, was found in Moslem Spain.'

Although other Spanish Muslim rulers like Abd al-Rahman II, Muhammad I and al-Hakam II had also achieved a tremendous amount and contributed greatly to the prosperity and progress of *al-Andalus*, it was during the glorious reign of Abd al-Rahman III that Islamic Spain reached its political, social, cultural and intellectual peak. His reign of forty-nine years was therefore a truly remarkable period in the history of Islamic Spain and Europe as a whole.

In less than half a century, he transformed a politically disunited and economically ruined country into one of medieval Europe's most dazzling and prosperous nations. As an enlightened, tolerant and generous ruler, he showered his subjects with wealth and gifts and they, in turn, revered him more than anyone else. Caliph Abd al-Rahman III died in Cordova at the age of seventy-one. *Al-Andalus* began to decline after his death and the Umayyads of Spain were eventually ousted from power in 1031 CE.

44

Abul Hasan al-Mas'udi (b.ca.895 - d.957 CE) / (b.282 - d.346 AH)

After the emergence of Islam in seventh century Arabia, the once ignorant and uncivilised Bedouins of the desert burst onto the global stage under the banner of their new faith and transformed the course of human history. The Arabs crushed the mighty Roman and Persian Empires and created for themselves one of the greatest empires in history. They also learned and understood the intellectual traditions of ancient Greece, Babylon, China and India. They now dominated human thought, culture and civilisation for more than a thousand years. As the Muslim world became a beacon of light for the rest of the world, people flocked to the foremost centres of learning and higher education in Baghdad, Damascus, Cordova and Cairo to study science, philosophy, mathematics, arts and architecture under the guidance of some of the Muslim world's greatest minds.

In doing so, Muslims prepared the way for the emergence of modern science, culture and civilisation. The tenth century was one of the most intellectually productive periods in the history of Islam. It was during this period that great Muslim thinkers like Abu Bakr al-Razi (see chapter 39), al-Farabi (see chapter 41), Ibn al-Haytham (see chapter 48), al-Biruni (see chapter 50) and Ibn Sina (see chapter 52) lived and succeeded. They collectively helped to push the boundaries of human thought and raise the search of knowledge to a new and higher level. Al-Mas'udi, the famous Muslim scholar and polymath, also lived during this period. He contributed immensely to the development of science, philosophy, Islamic history, geology, geography and natural history.

Ali ibn al-Husayn al-Mas'udi was born in Baghdad during the reign of the Abbasid Caliph al-Mu'tadid bi'llah (b. 857-d. 902 CE). His family traced their ancestry back to Abdullah ibn Mas'ud, the famous *Sahabi* (companion) of the Prophet, and thus were known to be a noble and respected Arab family. Al-Mas'udi grew up at a time when the influence of Mu'tazilism was still very strong within the intellectual and cultural circles of Baghdad. During his early days, he came under the influence of Mu'tazilism and, as a result, he became an outstanding interpreter of Islam from a Mu'tazilite perspective.

He was heavily influenced by the ideas of Mu'tazilite thinkers like Abu Ali al-Jubba'i and *Qadi* Abd al-Jabbar. He also became interested in history and the natural sciences. After completing his formal education, he left his native Baghdad and travelled extensively in pursuit of knowledge. He started his journeys relatively young. He was in his early twenties when he first began to travel in search of knowledge. Despite visiting and studying at all the main centres of learning in Iraq and the neighbouring Arab countries, his thirst for knowledge remained unquenched. Like Ibn Sina, al-Razi and al-Biruni, the continuous pursuit of knowledge and wisdom became his main occupation in life.

Although al-Mas'udi travelled the length and breadth of the Arab world, he did not travel for the sake of travelling. In fact, his journeys were motivated by a higher goal. Everywhere he went he carefully observed both the geographical and population makeup of the place and took abundant notes about the locals, their culture, traditions and social habits. At a time when even travelling from one town to another was a hazardous task, he became one of the great travellers in history. Three centuries before Marco Polo (b. 1254-d. 1324 CE) and Ibn Batutta (see chapter 73) were born, he travelled across a significant part of the then-known world on his own. From his native Baghdad, he journeyed across Persia and reached India while he was still in his twenties. In India, he visited the provinces of Sind, Punjab, Konkan and Malabar.

His detailed description of the area of Mansura, which was the business heart of Muslim Sind at the time, was vivid and enlightening. Mansura was named after Mansur al-Kalbi, the Umayyad governor of Sind. The city was situated on the banks of the Indus and al-Mas'udi considered it to be one of the most prosperous places he had visited in India. From India, al-Mas'udi retreated to Kirman in Persia, where he stayed for a period before returning again to India. This time he travelled further into India and, as he did so, he was surprised to meet Muslim traders and merchants who had sailed from as far away as Yemen and settled among the Hindus in some of India's most remote and isolated regions.

From India, he proceeded to Ceylon (present-day Sri Lanka) and from there he sailed down the Indian Ocean and reached Zanzibar and Madagascar. After a short stay in Madagascar, he set out for what is now the Gulf state of Oman, via Basrah. Then he sailed along the shores of the Caspian Sea and visited parts of Central Asia, Syria and Palestine before finally returning home to Baghdad. Eager to learn more, al-Mas'udi then travelled across the Middle East and Asia in pursuit of knowledge, and in the process, he became an original cultural explorer as well as a great geographer. He not only carefully observed all the places he visited but, most crucially, recorded his views and opinions about all these places in the form of a book which has remained in existence to this day.

As a great scholar and scientist, al-Mas'udi was not interested in gossip or hearsay. Rather he surveyed most of the geographical literature of his time – some of which he mentioned in his book by name – and did so to improve the historical, geological and geographical ideas and thoughts of his predecessors. Before him, some of the Muslim world's great thinkers and scientists (like al-Khwarizmi [see chapter 32], al-Kindi [see chapter 35] and al-Sarakhsi [d. 899 CE]) had researched and written extensively on these subjects. Indeed, al-Khwarizmi's celebrated book, *Kitab Surat al-Ard* (Book on the Shape of Earth) was a pioneering work in the field of geography which later inspired other Muslim scientists and geographers to pursue advanced research in this subject. Although al-Khwarizmi's book laid the foundations for the study of geography among the Muslims, it was al-Mas'udi who pushed the frontiers of geological and geographical knowledge. This was due to the fresh information and data he had obtained from across the world during his travels.

It was during his stay in Basrah that al-Mas'udi recorded his ideas and thoughts on a wide range of subjects including history, geology and geography in the form of a book. In his extremely large book, *Muruj al-Dhahab wa Ma'adin al-Jawhar* (The Meadows of Gold and Mines of Gems), he provided a detailed account of his travels in Persia, India, Ceylon and Central Asia. He also recorded new information about these places and highlighted their histories, geological variations and population structures. In addition to providing an informative description of all the places he visited, he compared and contrasted the traditions, cultures and habits of, for example, the Persians with those of the Indians.

In doing so, he paved the way for other Muslim thinkers, such as Ibn Khaldun (see chapter 75), to pursue their sociological analysis of culture and society. He then analysed the nature of earthquakes, geological formations and even explained how a windmill he had seen in the city of Sijistan (located in the Persian province of Khurasan) worked. The accounts of his journeys were accurate, vivid and comprehensive. A reader of this book cannot help but admire al-Mas'udi for his rigorous method, understanding of different cultures and varied interests. Equally remarkable was his ability to sift through such a large quantity of historical, geological, geographical and anecdotal information about so many different cultures and countries, before compiling them in the form of a book.

The book is considered to be one of the most comprehensive works ever written on the subject of history, geology and geography. Al-Mas'udi completed the first draft of his book in 947 CE. He later revised it in 956 CE and a French translation was published in Paris between 1861 and 1877 CE in nine bulky volumes. Al-Mas'udi's contributions in the fields of geology, geography and navigation were such that his pioneering works influenced prominent Muslim scientists and geographers like al-Biruni, al-Maqdisi (b. 945-d. 991 CE) and al-Idrisi (b. 1099-d. 1161 CE), better known in the Western world as Dreses. Many years later, most of the medieval Muslim geographers, like al-Idrisi, travelled across the Muslim world and parts of Europe, knowing only too well that pioneering scholars and explorers like al-Mas'udi had already preceded them many centuries earlier.

And although it is true that distinguished scholars and geographers like al-Idrisi broke new ground in the study of geography by developing cartography, which enabled them to produce the first accurate map of the world by representing its sphere in the form of a disc. However, a careful study of their work, especially al-Idrisi's famous, 'Entertainment for Those Who Wish to Travel Around the World', also known as *Kitab al-Rujar* (The Book of Roger), shows that their works were profoundly influenced by the geographical ideas and thoughts of al-Mas'udi.

In addition to being a pioneering explorer, a gifted geologist and an outstanding geographer, al-Mas'udi was also a historian of the highest calibre. Along with al-Baladhuri, al-Tabari, al-Isfahani, ibn al-Athir and ibn Khaldun (see chapter 75), he is today considered to be one of the Muslim world's greatest historians. Inspired by the Prophet of Islam, the early Muslims preserved as much information as possible about the *sira* (life and times of the prophet), his *sahabah*, and those of their *tabiun* (successors) for the benefit of future generations.

Al-Mas'udi followed in their footsteps and became a prolific writer and historian. Indeed, along with his great peers al-Tabari and al-Isfahani, he produced some of the most celebrated works of history ever written in Arabic. Like al-Tabari (see chapter 38), al-Isfahani (b.897 -d.967 CE) was an outstanding historian who wrote his *Kitab al-Aghani* (The Book of Songs) in more than twenty volumes. As a work of cultural history, this book is rated very highly by Muslim historians.

Like al-Tabari and al-Isfahani, al-Baladhuri (b.820 -d.892 CE) was another outstanding early Muslim historian who wrote two famous books, namely *Futuh al-Buldan* (The Conquest of Countries) and the voluminous *Ansab al-Ashraf* (The Lineage of the Nobles). In these two books, he provided a wealth of information about the early Islamic conquests, as well as detailed accounts of the life and times of the first four Caliphs of Islam and the Umayyad period.

However, unlike these historians, al-Mas'udi did not collect a large quantity of information and compile it in chronological order. Instead, he adopted a critical approach to writing and interpreting history. This is evident from the fact that his authoritative, 'The Meadows of Gold and Mines of Gems' surveys the same historical period as that of al-Tabari's book, yet his work is much superior to the latter in terms of quality of scholarship and literary production. Indeed, inspired by the critical and engaging historical methodology of the early Islamic historians such as al-Mas'udi, four hundred years later, Ibn Khaldun, the celebrated North African Muslim historian, authored his world-famous *Muqaddimah fi'l Ta'rikh* (Introduction to History).

Towards the end of his life, al-Mas'udi left Basrah and moved to Syria for a period. He then went to Cairo where he composed another voluminous work on history. Entitled *Akhbar al-Zaman* (An Account of Times), this work on history and culture consisted of around thirty volumes. In the final year of his life, he completed yet another important book, 'Book of Indication and Revision'. In this treatise, he explored aspects of human geography, climatology, oceanography, ecology, natural history and the philosophy of nature. Widely considered to be one of the greatest Muslim polymaths of all time across medieval Europe, al-Mas'udi became known as the 'Herodotus and Pliny of the Arabs'. He died at the age of sixty- two and was buried in al-Fustat in Egypt.

45

Al-Mutanabbi
(b.915 - d.965 CE) / (b.303 - d.354 AH)

Like Aramaic and Hebrew, Arabic is a Semitic language. However, unlike the other Semitic languages, Arabic is today a global language. As the common language of the Arab world, Arabic is the official language in almost all Middle Eastern and North African countries. As the language of the Qur'an and the linguistic medium of the Islamic civilisation, Arabic – like Greek and Latin – exerted a huge influence on the medieval world to the extent that it became the foremost language of science, mathematics, philosophy, arts, culture and scholarly communication during the glory days of Islamic civilisation. The Abbasid era is generally considered to be the Golden Age of Islamic science, philosophy and literature. During the reign of Harun al-Rashid (see chapter 28) and his son al-Ma'mun (see chapter 33) Baghdad became the world's main centre of philosophical, scientific and literary activities.

Once the language of the desert nomads, Arabic soon became the foundation of the Islamic civilisation – extending from Spain in the West to the Indus Valley in the East. At the time, the Arabs developed an impressive intellectual and literary culture which was very rich in both content and quality. Indeed, from pre-Islamic poetry to the Qur'an, and from the prose literature of Ibn al-Muqaffa (b. 724-d. 759 CE), al-Jahiz (b. 776-d. 868 CE) and Ibn Qutayba

(b. 828-d. 889 CE), to the brilliance of medieval Arabic poetry, the Arabs soon became the messengers of knowledge, wisdom and literature. Arabic poetry – otherwise known as *diwan al-Arab* (register of the Arabs) – also reached its peak during this period. Al-Mutanabbi was widely considered to be the greatest of all Arabic poets. He lived and thrived during this Golden Age of Arabic literature and poetry.

Ahmad ibn al-Husayn al-Jufi, better known as al-Mutanabbi (the would-be prophet), was born in the southern Iraqi city of Kufah. Originally from Yemen, his ancestors later moved to Kufah where they became prominent members of the Arab tribe of al-Kindah. Young Mutanabbi showed signs of intelligence and brilliant linguistic ability from an early age. He was born and brought up in a lower-middle-class Muslim family. He experienced considerable social and economic hardship as a child, but such unfavourable circumstances did not stop him from his studies. Indeed, while he was still a youngster, his family was forced to leave their home and stay for about two years on the outskirts of Samawa due to the Qarmatian uprising.

A faction of the Shi'a Isma'ili (Sevener) sect, the Qarmatians, emerged in the Iraqi city of Wasit during the latter part of the ninth century. From Wasit, they spread across eastern Arabia (al-Hasa) where they established a religious and utopian rule in 899 CE before making their presence felt in parts of Syria, Iraq and Khurasan. Politically speaking, they strongly opposed the Abbasids. But ideologically they were heavily influenced by a system of thought which incorporated elements of Gnosticism, Mazdakism and Shi'ism. In the beginning, the Qarmatians managed to start much social and political havoc across Iraq, eastern Arabia and Syria but eventually, they lost their momentum and declined in influence.

Chased out by the Qarmatians, al-Mutanabbi and his family lived in the safer region of known as Samawa where he polished his command of Arabic among the bedouins, who were renowned for their mastery of the language in its purest form. When he was about twelve, his family returned to Kufah where he began to compose poetry. His lack of formal education was however compensated for by his natural poetic skills and ability. Nonetheless, al-Mutanabbi was a passionate reader of Arabic poetry. He became thoroughly familiar with the works of his illustrious predecessors like Abu Nuwas (b. 756-d. 814 CE), Abu Tammam (b. 796-d. 850 CE) and al-Buhturi (b. 820-d. 897 CE). These celebrated Arabic poets lived and thrived in and around Baghdad during the early Abbasid period. Their poetic genius and literary ability endeared them to the ruling Abbasid elites who lavished money and gifts on them. Some even attained positions of power and authority.

For instance, Abu Nuwas was a celebrated poet who composed more than fifteen hundred poems on a wide range of subjects. At the same time, he was a close companion of the Abbasid Caliph Harun al-Rashid. Likewise, Abu Tammam and al-Buhturi were famous for praising leaders in their court. They enjoyed Caliphal support and were also known to have been very prosperous and wealthy individuals. Al-Mutanabbi not only read the works of these celebrated poets; he hoped to emulate them and become famous and wealthy himself. He began his poetic career in Kufah where he became popular after composing his early poems. Impressed with his poetic skills and ability, the local ruler became his first patron and supporter. This paved the way for al-Mutanabbi to reach the summit of Arabic poetry, although his road to success was not a smooth one and was loaded with considerable personal difficulties and hardship.

After leaving Kufah, he moved to Baghdad in 928 CE, where he experienced more personal and financial hardships. Indeed, the local people's failure to understand and appreciate his poetry made him very bitter and unhappy. The lack of response from the locals forced him to leave Baghdad and go to Syria, where he stayed for about two years. Here he earned his livelihood working as a freelance singer and entertainer. Hired by local government officials to perform on special occasions, he earned just about enough to live comfortably.

However, as an ambitious poet and performer, he was not happy with such a lowly position and was determined to rise to the peak of his chosen career. However, his failure to attain instant success had a considerable negative psychological impact on him. He could not understand why the masses failed to rate his poetry as highly as he did. This made him so unhappy, depressed and angry that he stopped working as a freelance singer and entertainer. He also became actively involved with the Qarmatians who at the time were engaged in a bitter political and military campaign against the Abbasids.

Inspired by the religious diversity and communistic philosophy of the Qarmatians, coupled with his lack of personal success and recognition, al-Mutanabbi began to sympathise with the difficulty of this religious sect. Like the latter, he was a passionate activist and a pessimistic thinker whose philosophy of life was gloomier than even the Qarmatians. Perhaps it was the similarities between his pessimistic view of life and the messianic philosophy of the Qarmatians which prompted him to join this group and champion their political and religious cause. However, according to some of his biographers, it was the troubles of the Qarmatians which profoundly moved him and so he decided to support them. Either way, he eventually became a fully-fledged member of this group.

Later, when the Syrian authorities arrested a group of Qarmatians and threw them into prison, al-Mutanabbi happened to be one of them. During his two-year imprisonment, he continued to improve his poetic skills. Soon after his release from captivity, he resumed his career as a freelance singer and entertainer. Thereafter, he travelled extensively via Damascus, Antioch and Aleppo, and entertained the masses with his songs and poetry. As a result, his reputation began to spread throughout Syria. This marked the beginning of his rise as a poet and performer. It was Badr al-Kashani, the governor of Damascus at the time, who recognised al-Mutanabbi's poetic talent and recruited him into his court. Soon he established himself as a famous court praiser at the age of twenty-nine.

Here he composed elegant verses in praise of the governor who rewarded him with both money and gifts. This, of course, made the other courtiers very jealous of him, so much so that he became the main target of their plots. Eventually, al-Mutanabbi was forced to flee for his life. He took refuge with the desert nomads on the outskirts of Damascus. But soon his fame reached the Hamdanid ruler Ibn Hamdan, known as Sayf al-Dawlah (Sword of the Dynasty), who recruited him to his famous court in Aleppo.

The Hamdanid dynasty (890-1004 CE) was established during the latter part of the ninth century by Hamdan ibn Hamdun and their rule extended from northern Iraq and Syria to Armenia in the north. The Hamdanid rulers were of nomadic Arab lineage. One of their rulers included Sayf al-Dawlah who ruled for more than two decades and became a very generous patrons of learning, art and architecture throughout their region. Under the patronage of Sayf al-Dawlah (b. 916-d. 967 CE), al-Mutanabbi's poetic talent finally began to flourish like never before. He stayed with the Hamdanid ruler for nearly a decade and during this period, he regularly accompanied him on his military campaigns. Since al-Mutanabbi considered Sayf to be a brave and noble Muslim warrior who was busy defending the Islamic world from its enemies, he never grew tired of praising and glorifying him.

Once, while Sayf was locked in a vicious but hopeless battle against the Byzantines, al-Mutanabbi composed many inspiring poems in praise of Sayf, which pleased the latter so much that afterwards he regularly called on him to sing verses to inspire his forces during military expeditions. As a master of the Arabic language, he composed poetry for all occasions and to suit all tastes. His way with words, emotional spontaneity and, especially, his ability to capture the mood of the moment has remained unrivalled in the history of Arabic poetry. For instance, referring to his patron Sayf al-Dawlah, he once wrote:

> 'Where do you intend, great prince? We are the herbs of the hills, and you are the clouds; we are the ones time has been miserly towards respecting you, and the days cheated of your presence.'

> 'Whether at war or at peace, you aim at the heights, whether you tarry or haste. Would that we were your steeds when you ride forth, and your tents when you alight!

> Every day you load up fresh, and journey to glory, there to dwell; and when souls are mighty, the bodies are tired in their search.'

> 'Even so the moons rise over us, and even so the great seas are unquiet; and our wont is comely patience, were it with anything but your absence that we tried. Every life you do not grace is death; every sun that you are not is darkness.'

In addition to traditional themes, al-Mutanabbi composed philosophical verses and love poetry. It is true that outstanding classical Arabic poets like Zuhayl (b. 520-d. 609 CE), al-Ta'i (b. 660-d. 743 CE), ibn Burd (b. 714-d. 784 CE), Abu Nuwas and Abu Tammam laid the foundations of early Arabic poetry, but it was in the works of al-Mutanabbi that Arabic poetry reached its peak and greatest glory. If ibn Burd was the father of Abbasid poetry and Ibn al-Muqaffa the pioneer of Abbasid prose, then al-Mutanabbi must be considered one of the most influential and gifted court praisers of all time. An outstanding poetic genius as he was, al-Mutanabbi was equally volatile and unpredictable; he liked his intellectual independence but frequently changed allegiance.

Yet his ability to champion goodness, boast about his self-importance, and mock and ridicule his opponents, while simultaneously displaying acts of generosity and kindness has continued to entertain and bemuse millions of fans of classical Arabic poetry up to the present time. As a Muslim and proud Arab, he was very fond of the history and symbolism of pre-Islamic Arabia, its culture and heritage. In his opinion, there was no contradiction between his Islamic faith and ancient Arabian culture and heritage. Not surprisingly, his poetry reflected nationalistic, philosophical, mystical, romantic as well as cultural themes. Like Abu Nuwas, he was a wise and cosmopolitan poet who lived his life to its full, experiencing its ups and downs, joys and sorrows in equal measure.

After a decade at Sayf al-Dawlah's court in Aleppo, al-Mutanabbi moved to Egypt for a period, before returning to his native Kufah. From Kufah he went to Baghdad and eventually settled in the Persian city of Shiraz, where he graced the court of the Buwayhid ruler Fanna Khusraw (b. 936-d. 983 CE), better known as Adud al-Dawlah, for a long time. Here he composed a large collection of poetry in praise of the serving ruler, who rewarded him handsomely for his poetic output. Ambushed by a group of desert bandits, al-Mutanabbi died at the age of around fifty while he was on his way to Baghdad.

But his poetry was of such a high quality that famous classical Arabic poets like Abul Ala al-Ma'arri (b. 973-d. 1057 CE) and al-Tha'alibi (b. 961-d. 1038 CE) were profoundly influenced by his works. Indeed, even some of the leading modern Arabic poets and literary figures like Badr Shakir al-Sayyab (b. 1926-d. 1964 CE), Taha Husayn (b. 1889-d. 1973), Nizar Qabbani (b. 1923-d. 1998 CE) and Ali Ahmad Sa'id Esber (b. 1930 CE), who is better known as Adonis or Adunis, have acknowledged their debt to al-Mutanabbi. In other words, his adventurous life, varied thoughts and inspirational poetry have continued to influence Arabic thought, culture and heritage to this day.

46

Abul Qasim al-Zahrawi
(b.936 - d.1013 CE) / (b 325 - d.404 AH)

After the Umayyads were removed from power by the Abbasids in 750 CE, Prince Abd al-Rahman ibn Mu'awiyah (see chapter 26) fled Damascus and arrived in North Africa. From there he reached Cordova, the capital of *al-Andalus* (Muslim Spain), and swiftly assumed control of that country. Abd al-Rahman's unexpected rise to power in Islamic Spain made certain the continuation of Umayyad rule in the Islamic West for almost another three hundred years. By unifying Spain under his able leadership, he also initiated one of the most memorable periods in European history. Under the guidance of his descendants such as Abd al-Rahman II (b. 792-d. 852 CE) and Muhammad I (b. 823-d. 886 CE), Spain became one of the most advanced European nations of the time.

During the reign of Abd al-Rahman III (see chapter 43) and al-Hakam II (b. 915-d. 976 CE), the fortunes of Islamic Spain increased so rapidly that Cordova became one of Europe's most impressive capitals. Thanks to their generous support of learning and higher education, Caliph Abd al-Rahman III and his successors turned Cordova into a thriving centre of intellectual, cultural and literary activities. As a result, scholars, scientists, mathematicians, philosophers and theologians flocked from across Europe to the leading Spanish cities to learn, study and master the finer points of their chosen subjects under the guidance of Europe's great minds. At the time, some of Europe's leading scientists, intellectuals and writers happened to be Muslims who flourished in Spain under the generous sponsorship of the Umayyad rulers. Al-Zahrawi was one such outstanding scholar and scientist whose contribution and achievement in the field of medicine and surgery was unique and unmatched.

Khalaf ibn al-Abbas al-Zahrawi, known in medieval Europe as Abulcasis, was born in the royal suburb of al-Zahra in Cordova during the glorious reign of Caliph Abd al-Rahman III. He was born and raised at a time when Islamic Spain was at its intellectual peak. Al-Zahrawi grew up to be a remarkably talented child who excelled in his studies. Thanks to Caliph Abd al-Rahman III's long and wise reign, political stability was restored across Muslim Spain and material prosperity spread throughout the country like never before. This encouraged both Muslim and non-Muslim scholars and scientists to collaborate and make some of medieval Europe's finest scientific and literary contributions, complementing the great cultural and architectural achievements of the time. After completing his early education in Arabic, and Islamic and physical sciences, al-Zahrawi developed a keen interest in the medical sciences.

Thus, he received advanced training in medicine at Cordova under the guidance of its leading Muslim physicians. He rapidly acquired an excellent reputation for his skills as a medical practitioner. It was during this period that Caliph Abd al-Rahman III came to hear about the young physician and he invited al-Zahrawi to the Caliphal court. Although he was barely in his mid-twenties at the time, the Caliph was deeply impressed by al-Zahrawi's profound knowledge and understanding of medicine and asked him to become his personal physician. He went on to serve the Caliph in the capacity of personal physician until the latter died at the age of seventy-one, having ruled Islamic Spain for no less than half a century.

As a physician, al-Zahrawi was a proud inheritor of traditional Islamic medicine. Ancient Greek physicians like Hippocrates, Galen, and Paul of Aegina were highly skilled medical practitioners who contributed immensely to the development of medicine. Gifted Muslim physicians like al-Kindi (see chapter 35), Ali al-Tabari and Abu Bakr al-Razi (see chapter 39) were the first to study and integrate ancient Greek medical thought into the Islamic worldview.

By doing this, they produced a powerful and authoritative medical combination which influenced the study and practice of medicine up to the modern period.

Although it is true that the Greeks considered medicine to be another scientific subject like astronomy and cosmology, the early Muslim scientists and physicians refused to separate science. Instead, they developed an integrated and holistic approach based on the fundamental principles and practices of Islam. That is to say, they were influenced by the principles of *tibb al-nabi* (Prophetic medicine). So the early Muslim physicians prepared an Islamic approach to medical science to remedy physical illnesses without ignoring the emotional and spiritual dimensions of humans. This explains why they organised their healthcare programme by following the all-encompassing Islamic approach to life, health and well-being. Following in their footsteps, al-Zahrawi also studied and practised medicine from a holistic perspective, and, like his illustrious predecessors, he believed that diseases and ailments were best treated in their wider context rather than in isolation.

Al-Zahrawi was barely twenty-five when al-Hakam II ascended the throne in Cordova and asked him to serve as his personal physician. Like his father, al-Hakam II was a wise, peaceful and compassionate ruler who became renowned for his love of learning and scholarship. To this end, he promoted learning and education across Muslim Spain and transformed the Academy in Cordova into one of the largest institutions of higher education in Europe at the time. Likewise, the libraries of Cordova were packed with books and manuscripts on all the sciences of the day. The Caliph also recruited some of the brightest minds of the time to his institutions of higher education and thereby blazed a trail which continued to burn across Europe for centuries.

Such was al-Hakam's enthusiasm for learning and scholarship that historians have compared him with the Abbasid Caliph Abdullah al-Ma'mun (see chapter 33) who was also an awesome champion of higher education and learning. As the Caliph's personal physician, al-Zahrawi had full access to his private library which contained some of the best medical textbooks of the day. This enabled him to devote all his spare time and energy to advanced study and research into all aspects of medicine. There were many other outstanding Muslim and non-Muslim scientists like al-Majriti, ibn Shabrut and Areeb al-Qurtubi who lived and practised medicine in Cordova at the time. But it was al-Zahrawi who was destined to carry out ground-breaking research in medicine and develop scores of new surgical tools and techniques for the benefit of future generations.

During the course of his medical career, al-Zahrawi not only followed theoretical research but also carried out practical experiments to demonstrate or confirm his theories at a practical level. As a pioneer of surgical anatomy, he performed a large number of operations, ranging from simple Caesarean sections to more complex and delicate eye operations. He performed such complex and often critical surgical operations at a time when there were no suitable medical tools or equipment to assist him. This prompted him to devise and develop the surgical equipment to perform medical operations with success, and in so doing, he laid the foundations for the modern science of surgery. No doubt the reluctance of the early Muslim physicians to carry out surgical operations hindered the development of clinical anatomy in the Muslim world until the pioneering al-Zahrawi took the initiative and invented the surgical tools necessary for performing operations.

He invented a large number of surgical tools and also performed numerous operations using the same tools and equipment. This paved the way for the emergence of surgical procedures and techniques as we know them today. Moreover, as a skilful practitioner of cauterisation (the practice of searing a wound by burning it with a hot iron to destroy the infection), al-Zahrawi was able to utilise this technique to treat other medical conditions such as haemorrhoids, malignant tumours and excessive bleeding. Medieval Muslim physicians preferred this method because traditional Islamic teachings justified it as a legitimate practice. Not surprisingly, al-Zahrawi recommended it for the treatment of apoplexy, epilepsy, bone fractures and dislocations, as well as various other surgical disorders.

As a practising Muslim, he understood and appreciated why women preferred to be operated on by women rather than men. So, he used to train midwives to carry out emergency Caesarean operations and other clinical procedures on women. If an operation turned out to be more difficult than anticipated, he provided guidance and instructions to the midwives from behind a screen.

In short, had it not been for al-Zahrawi, the Muslim contribution to the development of the science of surgery would not have been worth mentioning. After a lifetime devoted to medical research and surgery, al-Zahrawi eventually decided to write a book on the subject.

At the same time as al-Zahrawi was busy writing his book, Ibn Sina, (see chapter 52), the renowned Muslim physician and philosopher, was also in the process of writing his famous *al-Qanun fi al-Tibb* (The Canon of Medicine), which subsequently became one of the most popular medical encyclopaedias of all time. Like Ibn Sina's Canon, al-Zahrawi's monumental, 'An Aid to Him Who Lacks the Capacity to Read Large Books' played a decisive role in the development of modern medicine and surgical procedures and techniques.

Consisting of thirty chapters, this book was a massive encyclopaedia on medicine and surgery. Soon after its publication, it became one of the most sought-after surgical textbooks of its time. After providing a detailed and systematic explanation of cauterisation and how this medical procedure is to be carried out, al-Zahrawi explained how surgical operations, including ocular and dental surgery, should be performed using a scalpel. In addition to this, he covered obstetrics (childbirth) and explained how gallstones should be removed, among many other topics. He was of the opinion that a decaying tooth should be removed and, in certain circumstances, how it could be replaced with an artificial tooth, or one extracted from animals. As an accomplished dentist, he was thoroughly familiar with all aspects of oral hygiene and dentistry.

In the last part of his book, he provided a detailed explanation of bone fractures and dislocations. He argued that fractures and dislocations could be treated successfully without having to operate on them. For the first time in medical history, he correctly diagnosed that paralysis resulted from the fracture of the spine. He then explained all aspects of gynaecology (treating women's reproductive organs) including childbirth and also identified what is today widely known as 'Walcher's Position'. Most significantly, al-Zahrawi's book contained illustrations of around two hundred different surgical tools and equipment. Most of these were invented by himself, and all the illustrations were accompanied by a brief but precise explanation of each tool, its meaning and its purpose. The surgical part of his book became so popular in Europe that it was first translated into Latin by Gerard of Cremona and published in Venice in 1497 CE. Thereafter, it was published in Strasbourg in 1532 CE, Basle in 1541 CE and Oxford in 1778 CE. This book was rated so highly by the Europeans that it was prescribed to all medical students at Europe's leading universities until as late as the eighteenth century.

Though al-Zahrawi became famous in the West as the 'father of surgery', his works did not receive similar recognition in the Islamic East, perhaps because surgery was never a popular branch of medicine in the Muslim world. Nevertheless, al-Zahrawi was an unusually gifted physician who contributed more to the development of surgery and surgical tools and procedures than any other single individual in the history of medicine. He died at the age of seventy-seven and was buried in his native Cordova.

47

Firdawsi of Persia (b.cir 940 - d.cir 1020 CE) / (b.329 - d.411 AH)

The Persian people have played a central role in the development of Islam as a religion, culture and civilisation. During the early days of Islam, one of the close *Sahabi* (companion) of the Prophet was Salman al-Farisi, who was of Persian origin. But it was after the Muslim victory of Persia during the rule of Caliph Umar (see chapter 6), that the Persians embraced the new faith in great numbers. Proud of their glorious past and ancient Persian language, known as *Zaban-i farsi*, the people of Persia refused to abandon their culture and traditions in favour of those of their new rulers. Thus, the Persian language survived the Muslim conquest of Persia and, over time, it became the most important method of Islamic learning and scholarship after Arabic. Indeed, the Persians have contributed more to the rise of Islamic thought and culture than probably any other people.

This is most evident from the fact that some of the Muslim world's greatest scholars, thinkers and scientists like Abu Hanifah (see chapter 21), al-Bukhari (see chapter 36), al-Tabari (see chapter 38), al-Biruni (see chapter 50), Ibn Sina (see chapter 52), al-Ghazali (see chapter 56), Fakhr al-Din al-Razi (see chapter 63), and Nasir al-Din al-Tusi (see chapter 68), al-Baladhuri (b. 820-d. 892 CE) and al-Zamakhshari (b. 1075-d. 1145 CE) were all Persians. Their vast contribution to the development of Islamic thought and culture is in itself a testament to the greatness and resourcefulness of the Persian mind. And more than any other people, the Persians have produced some of history's most gifted poets and literary figures.

The Arabs produced the great poet al-Mutanabbi (b. 915-d. 965 CE). The Greeks produced Homer and the Indians produced the Rig-Vedic poets. The Persians honoured the Muslim world with some of its most celebrated poets, including Hafiz of Shiraz, Hakim Sana'i, Khayyam (see chapter 55), Rumi, (see chapter 69), Farid al-Din Attar and Jami. But Firdawsi is considered to be the leading light of Muslim poets. He was not only a man of unmatched poetic genius; he was also one of the greatest epic poets of all time.

Hasan ibn Ishaq, also known as Firdawsi, was born in the ancient Persian city of Tus located in the historic province of Khurasan. He was born into a well-to-do Muslim family and is said to have displayed great poetic ability even as a child. It is related that his father, Ishaq, was informed by a vision that his young son would one day grow up to be a famous poet. This prompted him to arrange for the boy to attend his local school to receive training in Persian language, literature and the religious sciences. Thanks largely to the generous support of its Samanid rulers, Tus had become a bustling centre of cultural and literary activities. Of Persian origin, the Samanids were appointed rulers of Transoxiana by the Abbasid Caliph al-Mu'tamid 'ala Allah during the ninth century. But later they separated the region of Khurasan and declared their independence from the Abbasids.

In so doing they founded the Samanid dynasty, which ruled from their capital in Bukhara located in modern Uzbekistan. The Samanids achieved their peak under the stewardship of Nasr II, who vigorously promoted learning and scholarship across his dominion. He offered generous support to eminent Persian scholars and poets. Although Nasr II died when Firdawsi was still a youngster, his successors also continued to promote learning and literary activities across the Samanid Kingdom, despite the political instability of the time. Firdawsi completed his formal education in Tus before commencing his career as a poet. As an enthusiastic fan of ancient Persian culture and heritage, he rapidly established his reputation as a poet, thanks to his unusual ability to versify Persian mythology and history.

It was during the reign of the Samanid ruler Mansur ibn Nuh (d. 976 CE) that the Turkish general Alptagin deserted from the Samanid army and established an independent kingdom in Ghazna, in present-day Afghanistan. Three decades later, the increasingly powerful Ghaznavids occupied a significant part of Samanid territory and thereby secured Ghaznavid power at the expense of their Samanid rivals. During this period of considerable political uncertainty and social disorder, Firdawsi polished his knowledge of Persian history and culture. He composed poetry which vividly described and recalled Persia's glorious past. When Sultan Mahmud, the famous Ghaznavid ruler, ascended the throne in 999 CE, Firdawsi was about fifty-nine years old. He had already started work on his poetic masterpiece, the *Shahnama* (the Book of Kings), which took him around thirty-five years to complete.

Unlike the Samanids, Sultan Mahmud of Ghazna was not a Persian; in fact, he was of Turkish heritage. Yet, like the Samanids, he became a generous patron of learning and scholarship. As a learned ruler, and one who had committed the entire Qur'an to memory, the Sultan preferred the company of the wise and the educated. Also, as a fan of Persian culture and poetry, he encouraged further research and scholarship in these subjects. During his successful reign of thirty-one years, he transformed the political and economic fortunes of his dynasty. He also recruited some of the most influential scholars, thinkers, writers and poets of the time to his capital Ghazna. Thus al-Biruni, the famous Muslim scientist;, al-Farabi, a great Islamic philosopher;, Unsuri (d. 1039 CE), a prominent linguist, and acclaimed poets like Farrukhi (b. 1000-d. 1037 CE) and Daqiqi (b. 935-d. 977 CE) all honoured his court.

After Firdawsi's fame began to spread far and wide, Sultan Mahmud sent him an invitation to come to his court in Ghazna. He was, of course, delighted to receive an invitation from one of the greatest rulers of his time. Sultan Mahmud's court became a major centre of poetic activity where outstanding literary figures such as Unsuri, Farrukhi and Manucihri (b. 1000-d. 1040 CE) lived and thrived. They enjoyed the generous support and hospitality of the Sultan, and in turn, they honoured Persian literature and poetry with their valuable contributions. When Firdawsi arrived at the court, he was received by the Sultan and his ministers with respect and honour. But the other court poets disliked his presence. They declined to entertain him until he first proved that he was worthy of their company. To become a member of this exclusive club of gifted poets, Firdawsi was required to produce Persian poetry of the highest quality, otherwise he would not be accepted as a member.

So, the court poets decided to put Firdawsi to the test. One day, while they were all sitting in the Sultan's garden chatting with each other, Firdawsi unexpectedly arrived. This prompted Unsuri to ask him to provide the finishing touch to a quatrain that he and his colleagues wished to compose. Firdawsi agreed to do so. Unsuri began: 'Your eyes are clear and blue as sunlit ocean'. Then Asadi added, 'Their glance bewitches like a magic potion'. Farrukhi continued, 'The wounds they cause no balm can heal, nor lotion'. Firdawsi then added the finishing touch, saying: 'Deadly as those love's spear dealt out to Poshan.' His response shocked the court poets. They were not expecting Firdawsi to know the ancient Persian story to which they were referring, but he did. They were very impressed. They showed their appreciation by embracing Firdawsi and praising him abundantly for his great poetic ability. Thereafter, he became one of the most talented and admired poets in Sultan Mahmud's court.

In Firdawsi, the Sultan found a poet who could accomplish a task which he had in mind, namely the writing of Persia's ancient history and culture in verses. By chance, Firdawsi had started to versify Persian history long before he arrived at the court of the Sultan. But now, encouraged by the Sultan who offered him a luxurious room in his royal palace, he decided to complete his poetic masterpiece. To keep him focused on his task, the Sultan announced that he would pay Firdawsi a gold coin for each completed couplet. In addition, he would give him a one-off payment of a thousand gold coins upon completion. Proud of his Persian culture and history, Firdawsi thus devoted all his time and energy to the composition of his monumental *Shahnama*. Consisting of around sixty thousand verses, in the *Shahnama*, he provided a detailed description of Persian manners, customs and ethics as well as military achievements and heroic episodes. He also included the religious practices and intellectual contributions of the Persian people from ancient times, up to the seventh century.

The *Shahnama* drew on information compiled and preserved during the time of the Persian Emperor Chosroe I. This information was then orally transmitted from one generation to another until Firdawsi versified it in a masterly fashion. Like the famous Indian epic *Mahabharata*, the *Shahnama* described historical events as well as mythical tales and stories. Even though the whole work was about the heroic deeds of Rustam and his family, Firdawsi's poetic imagination reaches its ultimate climax when he described how Rustam had accidentally killed his son, Sohrab. In Firdawsi's own words:,

'The story of Sohrab and Rustam now hear! Other tales thou hast heard: to this also give ear. A story it is to bring tears to the eyes, and wrath in the heart against Rustam will rise. If forth from this ambush should rush the fierce blast. And down in the dust the young orange should cast. Then call it just, or kind and unfair. And say we that virtue or rudeness is there?'

This tragic tale, versified so movingly by Firdawsi, today represents the height of Persian poetry. Before Firdawsi's time, many prominent poets like al-Muqaffa and Daqiqi had versified Persia's glorious past, but their efforts were surpassed by Firdawsi's great epic. After completing the *Shahnama*, Firdawsi visited Sultan Mahmud and gave him a copy of his poetic masterpiece. Delighted with his achievement, the Sultan offered him a camel-load of silver coins, rather than gold coins. Jealousy and political rivalry between different factions within the Sultan's court forced him to offer Firdawsi silver instead of gold, but Firdawsi was not impressed at all.

He was appalled by the Sultan's failure to keep his promise. Firdawsi then left Ghazna after having poetically ridiculed his former patron and benefactor. But this was not a wise move on his part because no other ruler of the time dared to entertain Firdawsi due to fear of revenge from Sultan Mahmud. Eventually, the reigning Abbasid Caliph, moved by his troubles, granted him shelter in Baghdad. Here, Firdawsi composed another influential work entitled *Yusuf-i-Zulaikha* (Yusuf and the Wife of Potiphar), wherein he versified the story of Prophet Yusuf as narrated in the Holy Qur'an.

Later on, Firdawsi became reunited with Sultan Mahmud and returned to his native Tus. As a gesture of goodwill, in 1020 CE, the Sultan sent him a camel-load of gold coins as he had originally promised. But when the camel train carrying the money entered Tus, the Sultan's men discovered that Firdawsi's funeral procession was already underway. He died at the age of eighty and was buried in his native city. The poet Asadi, who was a contemporary of Firdawsi, tried to imitate his poetic style but, as expected, he failed to produce anything comparable to the *Shahnama*. Even Matthew Arnold (b. 1822-d. 1888 CE), the nineteenth-century British writer and poet, was deeply inspired by the wonder that was, and still is, the *Shahnama*.

In short, if great poets like Hafiz of Shiraz, Umar Khayyam, Hakim Sana'i, Jalal al-Din Rumi, Farid al-Din Attar and Abd al-Rahman Jami were responsible for popularising Persian poetry, then the credit for laying the foundations of Persian poetry must go to none other than Firdawsi. As the national poet of Iran and author of arguably the greatest epic poem of all time, he was undoubtedly a great genius whose contribution to Persian poetry and literature has remained matchless to this day.

48

Ibn al-Haytham
(b.965 - d.1039 CE) / (b.354 - d.431 AH)

One of the oldest scientific subjects is astronomy. It studies celestial bodies such as the sun, the moon, the stars, the planets, the galaxies and every other object that exists in the universe. According to the historians of science, it was the ancient Babylonian, Egyptian, Chinese, Indian and Mexican people who first engaged in astronomical study and observation. But it was the ancient Greeks who made a serious contribution to the development of science in general and astronomy in particular. The Greeks produced many great astronomers including Thales, Pythagoras, and Ptolemy of Alexandria. One of the most popular works of Greek astronomy was the *Almagest* of Ptolemy. This essay was translated into Arabic by the early Muslim scholars and translators which enabled them to become thoroughly familiar with Greek scientific works.

However, following Ptolemy's death in 180 BCE, Greek science began to decline rapidly. But, thanks to the tireless efforts of the early Muslim scientists, ancient Greek science and astronomy were preserved. The Muslims also went on to create a complete Islamic scientific culture so that from the beginning of the eighth to the sixteenth centuries, Muslims led the rest of the world in scientific study. One of the most outstanding and influential Muslim scientists and a walking encyclopaedia of this period was Ibn al-Haytham.

Al-Hasan ibn Hasan ibn al-Haytham, known as Alhazen in the West, was born in the Iraqi city of Basrah during one of the most politically chaotic periods in the history of the Muslim world. The once unshakable Abbasid Empire was no longer a united and powerful entity. It had become divided into numerous independent kingdoms. Ibn al-Haytham was raised and educated in Basrah in the middle of the political uncertainty and social disorder. He studied Arabic language, literature and traditional Islamic sciences during his early years. He then received advanced education in literature, mathematics and astronomy, initially in Basrah and subsequently in Baghdad.

As the political capital of the Muslim world, Baghdad was considered at the time to be one of the world's major centres of scientific study and research. Under the generous support of successive Abbasid Caliphs, Muslim scholars, thinkers and scientists conducted research in all branches of the sciences; thus paving the way for the emergence of science and technology as we know them today. Following in the footsteps of the inventive early Muslim mathematicians and scientists, Ibn al-Haytham studied science under the guidance of some of the leading scholars and scientists of his day and became thoroughly familiar with mathematics, astronomy, physics and optics.

He attained such a mastery of science that his fame soon began to spread beyond the borders of Iraq. When the Fatimid rulers of Egypt came to hear about his scientific expertise, they invited him to move to Cairo and pursue his studies and research under their support. Given the political tension and uncertainty that gripped the Buwayhid regions at the time, Ibn al-Haytham was only too happy to move to Egypt because the Fatimids were famous for their generous funding for learning and higher education. After his move to Cairo, he was approached by the Fatimid ruler, Abu Ali Mansur (b. 985-d. 1021 CE) to devise a plan to control the excessive flooding of the Nile.

Although he knew this would be an incredibly difficult task, Ibn al-Haytham was not one to back down from a challenge. Thus, he made all the necessary preparations and began work on a flood -prevention plan. He soon realised the task was a multi-faceted problem that he could not solve alone. He therefore returned to the Fatimid ruler and explained the situation to him, but the ruler was not satisfied with his explanation. His failure to devise an effective flood-prevention plan cost him dearly as royal support was withdrawn from him. This forced him to sell copies of his books and manuscripts to pay for his daily expenses.

Along with medicine, mathematics and philosophy, astronomy was one of the favourite subjects of the early Muslim scholars and scientists. Before Ibn al-Haytham's time, prominent Muslim scientists like al-Farghani (Alfraganus), al-Khwarizmi (see chapter 32) and the Banu Musa Brothers (Muhammad, Ahmad and al-Hasan) among others had carried out extensive research in astronomy. In doing so, they contributed immensely to the development of astronomical knowledge across the Muslim world. The Muslim scientists dominated the study of astronomy during the medieval times and composed some of the most invaluable and authoritative works on the subject which were rated highly both in the East and the West right up until the modern period.

Unlike Ptolemy and other Greek astronomers, the Muslims adopted an empirical approach to the study of astronomy. They emphasised the importance of doing practical observations by using astronomical instruments to facilitate a better understanding of the celestial bodies. Not surprisingly, Ibn al-Haytham's work in astronomy was both practical as well as theoretical. He questioned and criticised existing astronomical knowledge and refused to accept the ideas of those before him at face value.

By adopting an experimental approach to the study of astronomy, he discovered how his predecessors had accepted aspects of Greek astronomical thought without critical study. In the process, he made many invaluable contributions, including carrying out a critical evaluation of Ptolemaic astronomy in 'The Summary of Astronomy'. In this book, he argued that the scientific methodology used by Ptolemy in his famous Almagest to explain the planetary motions was inconsistent and false. Instead, ibn al-Haytham proposed a fresh approach to the study of science and astronomy.

His convincing criticism of the Ptolemaic planetary theory later inspired other prominent Muslim astronomers, like al-Bitruji (Latinized: Alpetragius) of Islamic Spain and al-Shatir of Damascus to make fresh attempts to develop non-Ptolemaic planetary models. This, in turn, influenced the works of great Western scientists like Robert Grosseteste, Albertus Magnus, Roger Bacon, Regiomontanus, Nicolaus Copernicus and Johannes Kepler.

The move from Greek designs of imaginary heavens to one of a solid and observable physical reality (consisting of celestial bodies) was not only a radical shift in the study of astronomy but was also one of Ibn al-Haytham's major contributions to the study of science. This paved the way for his successors, especially those based at the famous Maraghah Observatory in Persia, to flourish and inspire famous Western thinkers and scientists like Galileo Galilei, Copernicus and Kepler to achieve as much as they did. Thus, it was not a coincidence that the planetary models developed by Ibn al-Shatir and Copernicus were later found to be virtually identical, differing only in minor details. Ibn al-Haytham authored more than twenty-eight books on all aspects of astronomy. There is no doubt that his astronomical thoughts greatly influenced both Ibn al-Shatir and Copernicus, thus contributing to the emergence of modern science.

If Ibn al-Haytham's contribution to astronomy was remarkable, then his works in the field of physics and optics were nothing short of astounding. Until recently, physics was widely considered to be a natural philosophy. Even Sir Isasac Newton (b. 1643-d. 1727 CE) considered himself to be a natural philosopher, rather than a physicist. In the same way, early Muslim physicists like al-Biruni (see chapter 50) and Ibn al-Haytham studied this subject as if it were a branch of natural philosophy, rather than physics as we know it today. Nevertheless, Ibn al-Haytham's contributions in physics, and especially in optics, were both original and hugely influential. As a scientific reformer, he formulated a new and unique 'experimental' approach to the study of science which was probably his most important and lasting contribution. That is to say, he developed and single-handedly championed an 'empirical' scientific method which emphasised the need for practical demonstrations of theoretical ideas and assumptions.

In other words, he was a pioneer of the scientific concept of hypothesis which must be confirmed by procedural or mathematical evidence. He developed an empirical scientific research method during his study of physics and optics. He did these five hundred years before the European Renaissance. This achievement firmly established his reputation as a great scientist and arguably one of the most influential physicists of all time. Not surprisingly, his *Kitab al-Manazir* (The Book of Optics) – written over a period of ten years from 1028 to 1038 CE – became the most sought-after book on the subject soon after its publication in 1038 CE. It was first translated into Latin in around 1250 CE and later reprinted many times throughout Europe. This book went on to exert a huge influence on prominent Western thinkers like Roger Bacon, Witelo or Vitello, Kepler and Newton, among others.

He is referred to as the 'father of modern optics'. In his book, 'The Book of Optics', Ibn al-Haytham moved away from the ideas of those before him and developed a new approach to optics based on his personal study and research. He discovered new knowledge in both optics and physiology. In this book, he dismissed the ancient Greek theory of vision. Light, according to the Greeks, emerged from one's eyes and then fell on an object to make it visible. Ibn al-Haytham was the first scientist to create a correct theory of vision. He explained that light emerged from a luminous object and then entered the eye to form an image, thus making the object visible. As an inventor of scientific 'experimentation', he proved his theory by carrying out several practical experiments and in the process also explored the anatomy and physiology of the human eye. He accurately explained the function of its various parts (including the conjunctive, iris, cornea and lens). He also diagnosed several diseases of the eye and suggested possible treatments.

Thereafter, he discovered and explained the laws of reflection and refraction in Book 4 of his Optics. He also provided an accurate explanation of the nature of atmospheric refraction. Ibn al-Haytham then discussed the purpose of numerous experiments he had conducted to acquire a better understanding of starlight, rainbows and different colours. By doing this, he discovered the principle of the camera obscura while observing the sun's image during an eclipse. Thanks to his scientific discoveries, the path was now shown for the developments of perspective in images and, ultimately, the ability to take photographs using a camera. Indeed, he studied and explained the principle of the camera obscura centuries before Kepler, Leonardo da Vinci and Newton wrote on the subject. After studying Ibn al-Haytham's *Kitab al-Manazir* (The Book of Optics), another renowned Muslim scientist, al-Farisi, wrote an extensive commentary on it under the title of 'The Review of Optics'. He wrote this book after repeating and improving many of Ibn al-Haytham's original experiments to clarify aspects of his scientific ideas for the benefit of future generations.

Ibn al-Haytham was not only an inventive astronomer and scientist, but he was also an outstanding philosopher, mathematician and physicist who contributed immensely to the development of a new scientific methodology. As a prolific writer and outstanding encyclopaedist, Ibn al-Haytham authored more than two hundred books on astronomy, physics, medicine and mathematics, in addition to several commentaries on the works of Galen and Aristotle. Indeed, his expertise in astronomy, physics and optics was such that he was considered to be one of the world's leading authorities on these subjects. After devoting his entire life to the pursuit of scientific knowledge and wisdom, he died at the age of seventy-four and was buried in Cairo. But, thanks to his remarkable scientific discoveries, humanity will forever remain indebted to this outstanding Muslim genius.

49

Mahmud of Ghazna (b 971 - d.1030 CE) / (b.360 - d.421 AH)

The Abbasids became the political leaders of the Muslim world after the downfall of the Umayyads in 750 CE. At that time, the Muslim world extended from Spain in the West to the banks of the Indus in the East. The Indus Valley was home to one of the world's first civiliszations. This was the area of modern-day Pakistan and Northern India. Some prominent Abbasid Caliphs like Abu Ja'far al-Mansur and Harun al-Rashid (see chapter 28) expanded the Abbasid rule. But their successes failed to maintain their grip on power. As a result, the vast Abbasi Empire broke up into smaller regional political lands. This was during the tenth century. The other major regional power of the time was the Ghaznavids. Alptigin, a charismatic Turkish military commander, had established them. Sebuktekin, who was a son-in-law of Alptigin, set up the first independent Ghaznavid territory in 977 CE.

Sebuktekin was a fearless military commander and a wise political administrator. During his rule of two decades, he strengthened Ghaznavid rule. He also established peace, order and security across his kingdom. Following his death in 997 CE, his young son Isma'il ascended the throne. He proved to be inexperienced and incapable. Isma'il was succeeded by his older brother, Mahmud. The Ghaznavids became one of Asia's most outstanding political powers under Mahmud's stewardship. They were also generous supporters of learning and education.

Mahmud al-Ghaznavi was born into a well-known Turkish family of soldiers and military leaders. His ancestors hailed from the steppes of Central Asia. The Abbasid rulers recruited his ancestors to strengthen their military might and power. Bold, fearless, and loyal, these recruits were offered military training to maintain their control. Their bravery, courage and loyalty soon won them the favour of the Abbasid rulers. Soon after they were promoted to the highest ranks of their armed forces. Mahmud's ancestors belong to this privileged group. They later came to use considerable political and military power within their localities. Mahmud's father, Sebuktekin became friends with the Samanids' leader Alptigin and married his daughter, who bore him a son. This son was Mahmud.

His mother educated him at home. Mahmud memorised the entire Qur'an during his early years. He was a talented student. He was an expert in Arabic language, literature, poetry, and traditional Islamic sciences. His father, who was a governor of Khurasan, was impressed by his son's intellectual ability and interest in learning. So, he trained him in the arts of political governance and military strategy. During this period, Mahmud served his father as his deputy. From this, he gained first-hand experience in political and civil management.

After his father's death, he overthrew his younger brother from power and ascended the Ghaznavid throne. He was only twenty-eight and, like his father, he was a wise and energetic ruler. Soon after becoming Sultan, he prepared his armed forces for his first military mission. In fact, within the first year of his reign, he overthrew the Samanids and defeated all the territories up to the Oxus. Oxus is the area that today covers parts of Turkmenistan, Uzbekistan, Tajikistan and Afghanistan. Up until this point, the Ghaznavid dynasty was restricted to the province of Ghazna in eastern Afghanistan and in parts of North-eastern Iran. However, under Mahmud's able leadership, it now received an unmatched political and military boost. By inflicting a crushing defeat on the Samanids, he proved his credentials as a military commander and gifted strategist.

A year later, he marched to Kohistan (meaning Highlands) – an area of hilly tracts in Pakistan and Afghanistan. He added this region to his expanding empire. He then turned his attention towards India. In 1001 CE, he launched his first military campaign against the Hindu ruler Jaipal I of Punjab. The two armies clashed near Peshawar. After a fierce battle, Sultan Mahmud's forces caused a crushing defeat on their enemies. Jaipal I was also captured during the battle.

Jaipal I was later released on the condition that he would not instigate any further attacks against the Ghaznavids. He had to pay an annual tribute to the Sultan. But Jaipal I violated the agreement soon after he was released by starting two further attacks against the Sultan's forces. On each occasion, he suffered a heavy defeat. Jaipal I then committed suicide as the defeats had distressed him. The victorious Sultan Mahmud went on to extend his regional control to the banks of the Indus. He was only thirty years old at the time and became the ruler of an empire which now extended from Central Asia to the Indus Valley. He did this from his political base in the eastern Afghan province of Ghazna.

Then, in 1002 CE, the Sultan captured the province of Sistan before preparing to cross the Indus. Two years later, he crossed the river with his large army and separated the region which is today known as Bhera. In the following year, he captured the towns of Ghur and Multan, and ousted its ruler, Dawud, from power. As expected, the Sultan's instant success against his enemies caused intense concern among all the Hindu rulers. They worried that the Sultan was getting too close to the regions for their comfort. Thus, the Hindu rulers united to create a confederation of Hindu territories to confront the advancing Ghaznavid emperor.

The combined might of the Hindu forces clashed with the Sultan's army in 1008 CE near modern-day Hazro. Anand Pal, the son of Jaipal I, led them. The Hindu group consisted of troops from across India including Gwalior, Kalanjar, Delhi and Ajmer. Likewise, Sultan Mahmud's army was an organised and disciplined fighting force. As expected, they fought with great skill and determination. In the ensuing battle, the Sultan's forces gained the upper hand and forced their rivals to flee. This was one of the major military victories of Sultan Mahmud's career. It enabled him to further extend Ghaznavid rule.

Mahmud was keen to take advantage. So, he quickly reorganised his forces and marched into Punjab in 1009 CE. He wanted to teach the unfaithful Anand Pal a lesson for breaking his agreement and for not paying an annual tribute to the Ghaznavids. Over the next decade or so, the Sultan faced tough opposition. The various Hindu factions made repeated attacks from both the land and the sea. Mahmud conquered his opponents on each occasion. In so doing, he extended Ghaznavid rule into mainland India. He established a permanent political and military base in Lahore, which became the capital of Ghaznavid Punjab. Then Sultan Mahmud strengthened his rule across the north-west of India including the province of Sind.

Then, in 1018 CE, the Sultan turned his attention towards the West. He quickly overthrew the Khwarizmshahs of Central Asia and the Buwayhids. In this way, he dominated Central Asia to such an extent that he became the definite ruler of that whole region. In the East, the Sultan fought a total of seventeen different battles against various Indian rulers, thereby establishing Ghaznavid supremacy across a large part of India. As a result, he soon became the most powerful and influential Muslim ruler of the eleventh century.

Some Hindu and Muslim historians have accused him of being a brutal, bloodthirsty and uncivilised military conqueror. But a balanced and impartial assessment of his life and career gives a different picture of the man who went on to establish an empire which would dominate Asian history for more than two hundred years.

The Sultan's Hindu critics misrepresented him because he disliked idolatry and crushed his challengers on the battlefield. As a practising Muslim, he considered the Hindu practice of worshipping and adoring idols wrong. However, he did not force the Hindus to reject their faith and convert to Islam. As a *hafiz* (one who committed the entire Qur'an to memory), he was aware of the clear Qur'anic order about the freedom to choose and practice one's faith. Thus, far from being anti-Hindu, he went out of his way to employ Hindus in his military and civil services. He even promoted them to positions of high power and authority. For instance, Tilak Roy and Soni were two of his most prominent Hindu military generals. They served him with great loyalty and distinction. Furthermore, a third of his army consisted of Hindus. Five out of his twelve senior generals were of Hindu background.

As a devout Muslim, the Sultan understandably had little sympathy for those who, having pledged loyalty to him, tried to betray him. For such people, he had no compassion. He punished them in an exemplary manner to deter others from doing the same. It is also true that on various occasions he attacked several Hindu temples. But to be fair to him, he did this out of political necessity rather than any other reason. As it happeneds, his Hindu opponents regularly stored gold as well as arms and ammunition inside the temples. They attacked his forces from there, so he had no choice but to retaliate. In the process, he damaged and destroyed several Hindu temples. Unlike many other influential Asian rulers, the Sultan was not a racist or a religious zealot. On the contrary, he tried to follow Islamic principles and practices to the best of his ability and did so both in times of war and peace.

That does not mean to say that he was innocent. No doubt he had his share of faults and made mistakes, and he would be the first person to accept this. As his early training was in Islamic theological and legal sciences, he genuinely tried to make things easier for his Muslim and non-Muslim subjects alike. In that sense, he was much wiser and more tolerant than many other great Asian rulers and conquerors. Indeed, Sultan Mahmud was not only a great conqueror; he was also one of Asia's most educated and articulate rulers. He transformed Ghazna, the capital of his vast empire, into one of Asia's most famous centres of learning and culture of the time. He was a generous sponsor of science, literary activities, art, and architecture. He constructed numerous beautiful mosques, colleges, libraries, fountains, and reservoirs throughout his empire, especially in Ghazna.

Thanks to his love of learning and education, Mahmud recruited some of the Muslim world's great scholars and thinkers to his court in Ghazna. Great Muslim scholars, like al-Farabi (see chapter 41), al-Biruni (see chapter 50) and others studied and researched science, mathematics, philosophy, history, linguistics, and comparative religion because of his generous sponsorship. As a result, they produced some of the most influential books. Interestingly, the poets who lived in his court competed to compose verses in praise of the Sultan to win his favour. Firdawsi (see chapter 47) was one such poet. He composed his monumental *Shahnama* (The Book of Kings) during Sultan Mahmud's reign and dedicated it to him. In appreciation of his efforts, the Sultan sent him a sack holding sixty thousand gold coins. Unfortunately, Firdawsi died before the caravan carrying the money reached his native town, Tus. Today the *Shahnama* is widely considered to be one of the greatest epic poems of all time.

Sultan Mahmud became a friend of the Abbasid Caliph in Baghdad to keep Islamic unity and solidarity. He first recognised the Caliph al-Qadir (b.947-d. 1031 CE) as the Caliph of all Muslims. Mahmud then re-established the practice of saying the Caliph's name in the Friday prayer sermon (*khutbah*) across the Ghaznavid lands. In response, the Caliph awarded him the grand title of 'Friend of the Commander of the Faithful and Right Hand of the State, the Faithful and the Community.' During his thirty-one-year reign, the Sultan completely rewrote the history of Asia and the Muslim world. He died at the age of around sixty and was buried in Ghazna in Afghanistan.

50

Al-Biruni
(b.973 - d.1051 CE) / (b.363 - d.443 AH)

The Prophet of Islam always encouraged his followers to seek knowledge from the cradle to the grave. To achieve this, he made the search of knowledge a compulsory commitment for all Muslims, both male and female. The Qur'anic verses and the Prophet's sayings, therefore, generated tremendous interest, enthusiasm and love for learning within the early Muslim community. This, in turn, prompted the early Muslim scholars, thinkers and writers to devote their entire lives to learning and spreading knowledge. 'Knowledge', said the blessed Prophet, 'is the lost property of the believer, so let him learn it up wherever he finds it.' Very few Muslim scholars and thinkers followed this Prophetic advice more rigorously than the industrious and remarkably gifted al-Biruni.

Muhammad ibn Ahmad al-Biruni was born near the city of Khwarazm in the Central Asian province of Khurasan. As the birthplace of some of Islam's greatest scholars, thinkers and scientists, Khurasan at the time was a very large and thriving province. Though his real name was Muhammad, he became famous by his surname, al-Biruni. He was born and brought up in an intellectually friendly environment. Young al-Biruni pursued his early education in Arabic and Persian languages, before receiving training in traditional Islamic sciences, literature and the physical sciences.

From an early age, he became interested in mathematics and the physical sciences. He acquired knowledge of the religious sciences under the guidance of important local scholars. For many years al-Biruni studied the physical sciences under the guidance of famous authorities and distinguished astronomers and mathematicians of his time. He was also a prominent student of the popular Muslim astronomer and scientist Abul Wafa Muhammad al-Bujzani.

Abul Wafa was based at the celebrated *Bait al-Hikmah* (the House of Wisdom) in Baghdad and became an astronomer *par excellence* and authored more than a dozen books on the sciences of his time. According to some historians, al-Biruni also studied under Abul Wafa's guidance. The majority of historians dismiss this view as he died in 993 CE when al-Biruni was around twenty. Since al-Biruni was still living in Central Asia at the time, most historians say it was very unlikely for him to have met or studied by this great astronomer.

It was not until 995 CE that al-Biruni began to travel in pursuit of knowledge. During this period, he visited some of the most prominent centres of learning in Central Asia, before finally settling down in the Persian city of Jurjan. He worked for its present then ruler, Shams al-Ma'ali. He lived here for more than a decade and pursued advanced study and research in all branches of science and mathematics. At the age of twenty-seven, al-Biruni wrote his acclaimed book 'A Treatise on the Chronology of Ancient Nations'. In this treatise, he explored the nature and concept of time in the light of historical evolution and change, focusing on the lives and times of the ancient people and their fate. By developing an interesting and illuminating analysis of historical progression and geological changes, he was able to evaluate how such changes impacted the lives of ancient peoples.

In this book, he also analysed and disproved, the views of those philosophers who considered time and creation to be eternal. Rather, he argued, historical evidence and changes in the earth's geological formation proved, if proof was required, that time and creation were finite. This argument, prepared by al-Biruni, repeated the Qur'anic view on this matter. That is to say, only Allah is infinite and eternal, while His creation is finite and temporal. Since he was a keen student of the Qur'an, it is not surprising that al-Biruni's intellectual worldview was heavily influenced by the Qur'anic concept of Allah, creation and time.

In 1012 CE, al-Biruni returned to his native Khwarazm where he resumed his studies into different branches of learning under the guidance of Abd al-Samad al-Awwal, who was a leading scholar of his time. While he was busy pursuing his studies, the political situation in Central Asia began to suddenly change for the worse. The rulers of the different Central Asian kingdoms fought each other for political and military dominance. This state of affairs continued until the Ghaznavids appeared on the political scene, under the able leadership of Sultan Mahmud (see chapter 49), and took overall control of the region. The Sultan marched into Khwarazm and occupied it and the surrounding region. He took al-Biruni and his tutor Abd al-Samad al-Awwal back to Ghazna as captives.

Abd al-Samad was charged and found guilty of deviation and sentenced to death by the ruling elites. Al-Biruni's life was saved by the timely intervention of the Sultan's chief advisor. Al-Biruni was already widely recognised as a distinguished scholar and scientist. So Sultan Mahmud did not want to lose a scholar of his calibre. For this reason, he appointed him as his senior astronomer and scientific advisor. Hereafter, he regularly accompanied the Sultan on his journeys and military expeditions. Al-Biruni personally disliked warfare – and often expressed his profound reservations about launching military expeditions to foreign countries, especially the Sultan's repeated invasions into India. He persuaded Sultan Mahmud to preserve some of India's most ancient cultural and religious heritage. In other words, al-Biruni was not only a great scientist and intellectual, but he was also a cultured individual who loved and admired different languages, traditions and cultures. Thus, he was very keen to preserve ancient Indian cultural heritage for the benefit of future generations.

He stayed in India from 1021 to 1031 CE and during this period, he devoted all his spare time and energy to the pursuit of knowledge and wisdom. Despite being recognised as an all-round walking encyclopaedia who knew more about mathematics, astronomy, physics, medicine, chemistry, biology, history, philosophy, geography, geology, literature, poetry and religion than probably any other scholar of his time, he was eager to study and learn Indian sciences. Indeed, it would not be an exaggeration to say that al-Biruni was one of the most learned and gifted Muslim intellectuals of all time. His ability to learn and retain information on such a wide range of subjects and assimilate them to create a powerful intellectual mixture was almost unequalled. Just as a sponge sucks up water from a surface leaving it clean and dry, so al-Biruni's brain absorbed knowledge.

Although during the early part of his life, he specialised in mathematics, physics and astronomy, he later developed a considerable interest in other scientific subjects such as chemistry, optics, pharmacology and medicine. His enthusiasm for religious, cultural and linguistic studies, as well as the social sciences, continued to increase as he matured. When he arrived in India, he quickly mastered Sanskrit, the common language of ancient India. It exposed him to the treasures and wisdom of the Indian civilisation. He studied anything and everything he could lay his hands on and became thoroughly familiar with Hindu religion, culture and traditions.

As one of the first Muslim scholars to travel to India and study there, al-Biruni was in a unique position to learn Sanskrit and undertake a decade-long wide-ranging study of, and research into, ancient Indian languages, culture, history, geography, religion and philosophy. The outcome of this research was his monumental *Kitab Ta'rikh al-Hind* (The History of India). It is today considered to be a unique source of information about ancient India and a pioneering contribution to the study of human culture and civilisation. Written by one of the Muslim world's brightest minds, it was one of the first books to be composed about inter-civilisational studies and dialogue. A quick browse through this book is sufficient to prove that al-Biruni acquired an intimate knowledge and understanding of Indian thought, culture and history. Indeed, his knowledge of India's geography and demographic makeup was both extensive and authoritative.

After surveying India's different climatic conditions and demographic patterns, he measured the size and distance of its major towns, cities and rivers with remarkable accuracy. He was also the first scholar to point out that the region known as the Indus Valley consisted of largely delta land during the prehistoric period, which modern scientific research has confirmed as an accurate assessment. Moreover, al-Biruni played a pivotal role in the translation of ancient Indian texts into Arabic and *vice versa*. For instance, he was one of the first to translate Euclid's *Elements* and Ptolemy's *Almagest* into Sanskrit. His translation of the *Yoga-sutras* of Patanjali from the original Sanskrit into Arabic has survived to this day. His other books, including 'The Book of Civilisation', are filled with facts, figures and quotations from some of the most revered religious texts of Hindu dharma, including the *Bhagavad-Gita*. This proves that al-Biruni was thoroughly familiar with the religious beliefs, customs and practices of the Hindus.

As an outstanding fount of knowledge and prolific writer, al-Biruni wrote a large number of books and essays. The exact number of his works is not known because most of them are no longer available. However, according to some historians, he wrote one hundred and eighty books, while others suggest the number may be closer to two hundred books. His most famous books include, 'The Book of General Knowledge' and 'The Determination of the Co-ordinates of the Cities'. In these books, he provided a systematic analysis of a wide range of subjects including astronomy, cultural history, comparative religion, geology, philosophy and geography.

His sharp intellect, combined with his immense learning and remarkable linguistic skills, enabled al-Biruni to learn, assimilate and master knowledge from many different sources and write efficiently and authoritatively on almost all the sciences of his day. So much so that it is not possible to put al-Biruni into any one category of learners of knowledge. His learning and education encompassed such a wide range of subjects that he resists being classified. It is remarkable how one person could have acquired so much knowledge within such a short lifespan, yet that is precisely what al-Biruni achieved. Most interestingly, despite being fluent in Persian and Sanskrit, he chose to write mainly in Arabic, perhaps because that was the *lingua franca* of the Islamic world at the time.

As a devout Muslim, al-Biruni never compromised his Islamic beliefs and practices in the pursuit of his scholarly aims and objectives. Unlike many other great Muslim scholars and thinkers like Ibn Hazm (see chapter 53), al-Shahrastani (b. 1086-d. 1158 CE) and Ibn Taymiyyah (see chapter 72), his approach to the study of comparative religion was neither sectarian nor eclectic. He had a profound respect and regard for all the world's great religions, cultures and traditions. Being a wise and tolerant writer and intellectual, he had no interest in the intra-Islamic sectarian conflicts which prevailed between the Sunnis and Shi'as at the time. According to some historians, he was a Sunni Muslim who had a profound knowledge and understanding of the *Sharia* (Islamic law) from the Sunni perspective.

In other words, al-Biruni preferred to focus more on the universal dimension of Islam than engage in petty and often fruitless theological or doctrinal hair-splitting. To him, Islam was a universal faith and message which sought to unify people of different racial and cultural backgrounds, rather than divide them. Thus, he was in the habit of constantly emphasising the oneness of our common humanity. The never-ending pursuit of knowledge was more important to him than anything else because it enabled a Muslim to acquire an in-depth understanding of his own faith, and also promote the need for greater awareness and understanding of religious and cultural diversity. In so doing, he hoped to foster inter-religious and cross-cultural understanding and tolerance between people of all backgrounds. In short, al-Biruni was not simply an outstanding visionary; he was also one of the great developers of inter-civilisational dialogue and understanding.

When he was around fifty-eight, he left India and returned to Ghazna where he received a warm reception from Mas'ud, Sultan Mahmud's son and successor. It was under the support of the new Ghaznavid Sultan that he composed most of his books. His famous *al-Qanun al-Mas'udi* (The Canon of Mas'ud) on the subject of astronomy, which – as the title of the book suggests – was dedicated to Sultan Mas'ud. The Sultan was profoundly impressed by it and sent him an elephant loaded with silver coins. Al-Biruni politely returned the gift, saying he served knowledge out of love rather than for material benefit.

Al-Biruni spent the rest of his life in Ghazna and passed away at the age of seventy-eight. Unlike al-Kindi (see chapter 35), Abu Bakr al-Razi (see chapter 39), al-Farabi (see chapter 41), Ibn Sina (see chapter 52) and al-Ghazali (see chapter 56), the works of al-Biruni were not translated into European languages until relatively recently. As a result, his ideas and thoughts did not receive much circulation in medieval Europe. By contrast, in the East, he is revered as one of the Muslim world's most influential thinkers and polymaths, so much so that in the intellectual history of Islam, the period from 973 to 1051 CE is known as the 'Age of al-Biruni'.

51

Karima al-Marwaziyya (b.ca.975 - d.1070 CE) / (b.365 - d.442 AH)

Karima was the daughter of Ahmad ibn Muhammad al-Marwaziyya. She is given special attention because of her religiousness and influence on *Hadith* scholarship. She is one of the first famous narrators of *Hadith* to appear in the historical records after an absence of women for a long time. She was a distinguished female scholar of the *al-Jami' al-Sahih* of Imam al-Bukhari, the most authentic book on *Hadith* (see chapter 36). In other words, she was a great *muhaddithah* (a female expert of *Hadith*) of her time. She is also well known for combining both knowledge and piety in her personality. Karima was born in a village known as Kushmihan, close to Merv in Turkmenistan in the second half of the fourth/tenth century. She was lovingly known as Umm al-Kiram, meaning 'mother of the generous'.

Merv was a stylish and cultured city which attracted scholars from all over the Islamic world. People came to study in its magnificent libraries and take part in one of the greatest knowledge exchanges in the medieval world. Karima grew up in an incredible scholarly community. One of these great scholars was Karima's teacher. His name was al-Kushmihani and he was a master of the *Sahih* of al-Bukhari. He had learnt it from his teacher, Abu 'Abd

Allah al-Firabiri, who had heard it from the great Imam al-Bukhari directly twice. This means that al-Kushmihani had an extremely short *isnad*. An *isnad* is a chain of transmission of a *Hadith*. The shorter the *isnad* one has, the closer they were to the author and Prophet Muhammad. Karima accurately learnt the *Sahih* al-Bukhari from al-Kushmihani. She was twenty-four years old when he died. In other words, Karima's reputation rested on her transmission of this major *Hadith* book with only two links between her and the writer himself. This meant that she had a lofty *isnad*. However, some have questioned her hearing from al-Kushmihani. They suggested that her father would bring her to al-Kushmihani's lessons while she was still too young to understand traditions.

Her only biographer, who lived when she was alive, al-Farisi, has praised her. Karima was a chaste, virtuous, and well-known woman. Al-Farisi also reports that she narrated the *Sahih* of al-Bukhari on the authority of al-Kushmihani. She had also heard *Hadith* from Imam al-Sarakhsi and other teachers of his generation. As a certified *muhaddithah*, this meant that Karima had a rare expertise. She could teach and narrate *Hadith*. Al-Farisi says that he was given *ijazah* (permission) for the works that she had heard and that is why al-Farisi reported *Hadith* on her authority.

Before establishing herself as a teacher, she went on an amazing journey. She searched for knowledge by following Islamic rules. She did not travel long distances without her father, Ahmad, to learn the sayings of Prophet Muhammad. Travelling was not easy in those days. Karima had to sacrifice all her comfort. She was strong-willed and she was patient with the difficulties she experienced during this challenging and life-changing journey. On their way, they visited Sarakhs and Isfahan in modern-day Iran. These cities were famous for their libraries. Then they travelled to Jerusalem, which was at that time under Islamic rule. Finally, they reached Makkah. At the time Makkah had very few female *Hadith* scholars who were well-known and distinguished.

Karima had learnt the *Sahih* by heart and had studied in many libraries in many cities. She must have been delighted to arrive in Makkah where the Prophet had lived. Al-Farisi also notes that Karima eventually settled in Makkah and established herself as a *muhaddithah*. She taught it many times exactly as she had received the text from her teachers. She attracted students very quickly because she had a strong *isnad* and was meticulous as a teacher. Moreover, she had set very high standards for her students to pass before she permitted them to transmit the *Sahih*. Soon her reputation spread far and wide. It is unclear whether scholars studied with her in assemblies in mosques or privately in her house. Her biographers praise her and regard her in high respect for her intense worship of Allah, her piety and for being an upright woman. Imam Al-Dhahabi noted that Karima possessed knowledge and understanding. She was a good person who worshipped regularly.

They also record that Karima remained unmarried and devoted herself to religious study. She is said to have followed the *Hanafi madhhab*. Like other scholars who lived in Makkah, many pilgrims searched for her to gain her certification. For example, the *Maliki* jurist al-Tulaytuli (of Toledo in Spain) heard *Hadith* from her when he was in *hajj*. The celebrated *Hadith* scholar (*muhaddith*) of Spain, Abu Bakr Muhammad ibn Sabaq Saqli was a committed student of hers. He had gone to Makkah after Muslims lost Sicily and learn *Hadith* from Karima. After returning he settled in Granada, Spain where he taught *Hadith*. Other transmitters from her were from places such as Egypt, Kufa, Qazvin and Hamadhan. An outstanding scholar, al-Dhahabi, has an interesting incident to tell. A scholar wrote down seven pages from Karima's copy of the *Sahih*. When he wanted to compare his copy against hers by himself, she refused. She insisted that she would review it with him. This made sure that there were no errors in the transmission because her reputation as a *Hadith* scholar depended on the quality of her *isnad*. This is how she ensured that her students did not make any mistakes. Al-Dhahabi also mentions another incident from al-Hamdani, who went for *hajj*. Unfortunately, al-Hamdani received news of her death on his way to Makkah. He was unable to fulfil his wish to meet Karima and get permission to transmit *Hadith* from her.

Karima spent much of her time and effort in teaching the Sahih as she had learnt it from her teachers. Another incident is reported by al-Sam'ani who notes that al-Khatib read the whole of *Sahih al-Bukhari* to Karima in five days. Likewise, al-Yafi'i also remarks that she was precise and had the correct understanding of her transmissions. She was also outstanding in *Hadith* circles. Her biographers agree that her reputation in *Hadith* circles was based on her accurate teaching of the *Sahih*. But also, pilgrims arriving in Makkah for their *hajj* came to learn from her and took her knowledge back to Toledo, Baghdad and other Islamic cities. The biographies show that her reputation was well recognised as she attracted many famous *Hadith* transmitters to her assemblies. These included the Shaf'ī scholar al-Khatib al-Baghdadi and al-Sam'ani, a *Hanafi* scholar. Many other leading scholars of Baghdad were among her students. Al-Khatib may have taken her reputation to Baghdad. This meant that Karima had created a large network of students, teachers and *'ulama* in some major urban centres.

Over the centuries, there began a practice of bringing very young children to the assemblies of aged *shaykhs* nearing death. This enabled the shortening of *isnad*s, which were growing ever longer over time. However, she lived longer than most other famous and reliable transmitters, who were also the students of Al-Kushmihani. This explains why Karima had gained such an exceptionally high rank. Al-Dhahabi mentions that she died when she was nearly 100 years old. Moreover, Karima was in her late twenties when several of her well-known teachers died. Her longer life enabled her to become a valuable link between the old and young generations of scholars.

Karima was a celebrated and trustworthy transmitter of one of the most authentic books in Islam. Her name is at the top amongst the best and most famous narrators of *Sahih al-Bukhari*. Karima's copy of the *Sahih* was held in higher value than the copies of some other male scholars of her time. She set a trend for future students, especially females women, in showing how to teach and transmit sacred knowledge. Karima became a model to show that women could learn and repeat long texts with precision. As you have read in the story of Aishah, many *Hadith* have been protected by women companions of the Prophet. Karima and other *Hadith* scholars followed in their footsteps and established themselves as reliable *Hadith* scholars. She was not originally from Makkah. But she is known as a Makkan scholar because she settled and died in Makkah and also because she brought a wealth of great knowledge to Makkah. The legacy of Karimah is unequalled and her life has much to offer all Muslims of all times to come.

52

Ibn Sina
(b.980 - d.1037 CE) / (b.370 - d.429 AH)

Modern Western scientific thought and culture owe a huge debt to the early Muslim philosophers, scientists and thinkers who, by the strength of their characters, intellectual brilliance and powers of imagination, lit up human thought, culture and civilisation like never before. The Muslim contribution to the study of philosophy and medicine was such that it opened the way for the rise of modern scientific thought. Indeed, humankind's achievements in these subjects were ancient and very limited when compared to the dazzling contributions the early Muslims made in these fields of human thought.

But our failure to show our appreciation and acknowledge our debt to those remarkable early Muslim philosophers and scientists only reflects negatively on us. One man who dominated the field of philosophy and medicine more than probably anyone else in the history of human thought was Ibn Sina. He is known in the West as Avicenna. This great and hugely influential Muslim philosopher and physician ignited an intellectual path which continues to burn to this day.

Husayn ibn Abdullah ibn Hasan ibn Ali ibn Sina was born in Afshanah, a small town located close to Bukhara, in Uzbekistan. As the capital of the ruling Samanid dynasty, Bukhara was a busy centre of learning and business. Originally from Balkh, Ibn Sina's father, Abdullah, moved to Afshanah where he met his Persian wife, Sitara, and became a prominent member of the Samanid civil service. His second son, Husayn (better known as Ibn Sina), was born a few years later. When Ibn Sina was around five, his family left Afshanah for Kharmayathnath, a town located on the outskirts of Bukhara, where his father became governor. Abdullah, Ibn Sina's father, was a very learned and cultured man who ensured his son received a thorough education in both the religious and philosophical sciences.

According to the custom of the day, young Ibn Sina committed the whole Qur'an to memory before he was ten and became thoroughly familiar with the traditional Islamic sciences. He was blessed with an amazing memory and gifted intellect;, he read all the religious, philosophical and scientific literature available to him in his locality. His ability to read rapidly and understand complex ideas with ease enabled him to acquire a comprehensive knowledge of *fiqh* (Islamic jurisprudence), *mantiq* (logic), mathematics, *falsafah* (philosophy), medicine and astronomy. Indeed, he was able to engage in heated debates with some of the most learned scholars of his time even, before he reached his eighteenth birthday.

Such was his thirst for knowledge that he read and became thoroughly familiar with, al-Farabi's huge commentary on Aristotle's metaphysics before he was eighteen. His vast knowledge of all the sciences of his day soon made him a popular figure in his locality. It was also during this period that the ruling Samanid monarch, Nuh al-Samani, was taken seriously ill. None of his court doctors were able to cure him. But after Ibn Sina's fame as a skilled medical practitioner reached the corridors of power, he was asked to treat the sick monarch.

He not only diagnosed the illness, but he also successfully treated it and restored the monarch to full health. The Samanid ruler was greatly impressed with the young doctor and gave him the keys to his private library. Ibn Sina found enough religious, philosophical and scientific literature to keep him occupied for a long time. Being an unselective reader, he studied everything he found in the library and became a master of medicine, philosophy, logic, theology and literature. After he was convinced of his superior intellectual ability and maturity of thought, he began to write in large quantities. In addition to an essay on mathematics, he authored a book on ethics and also compiled an encyclopaedia of all the sciences of his time. Astonishingly, he was only twenty-one when he composed these books. He was admired by politicians and the public alike for his learning, scholarly achievements and medical skills. He quickly became a celebrity in his locality.

However, he lived in an unstable period in the history of Muslim Central Asia. So Ibn Sina also became a victim of the mindless political rivalry and military hostility that the various Muslim rulers of that region had against each other. Following the death of his father, he left his hometown and moved to Jurjaniyyah, where he received a warm welcome from its ruling elites. Ibn Sina did not stay here for long, but his time in Jurjaniyyah proved very productive from a literary point of view. During this period, he composed two more books on mathematics and astronomy. He was then forced to leave the city due to the growing power of the great Ghaznavid ruler Sultan Mahmud (see chapter 49).

For the next nine years, Ibn Sina was compelled by the unfavourable political circumstances of the time to travel from one place to another. During this period of travel and political uncertainty, Ibn Sina found time to write his philosophical masterpiece, *Kitab al-Shifa* (The Book of Healing), in eighteen volumes. He wrote his famous medical encyclopaedia, *Kitab al-Qanun fi al-Tibb* (The *Canon* of Medicine), in another fourteen volumes. On one occasion, he even served as a Minister in the court of the Buwayhid (or Buyid) monarch Shams al-Dawlah. He fell out with the monarch's son who imprisoned him for four months. After escaping from captivity by disguising himself as a Sufi dervish, he fled to Isfahan which is in modern-day Iran.

The peace and tranquillity of this city was a breath of fresh air for him. He spent the next fifteen years of his life here writing and doing academic research. He completed many other highly-rated books and essays. Isfahan was at that time a renowned centre of learning and scholarship. It is not known exactly how many books Ibn Sina wrote in total since a large number of his works have been destroyed, including his ten-volume Arabic Dictionary. However, around two hundred and fifty books and treatises have survived.

By all accounts, Ibn Sina was a multitalented genius whose scholarly interests covered all the major branches of learning known during his lifetime. But it was his decisive contribution to the fields of medicine and philosophy which earned him universal fame and recognition. His achievements in medicine were such that it is not possible to speak about them except in superlatives. His *Kitab al-Qanun fi al-Tibb*, which became known throughout the Western world as the *Canon*, is considered by medical historians to be one of the greatest medical encyclopaedias of all time. As the Bible of medieval medicine, it was a compulsory textbook for all medical students at the leading European universities until as late as the eighteenth century.

In the East, however, it continues to be used as a standard work of reference by the practitioners of traditional medicine to this day. As it happens, Ibn Sina's popularity as a medical writer and thinker was such that he became known as the 'Prince of Physicians' throughout medieval Europe. His *Canon* became one of the most famous textbooks in medical history. It is divided into five main chapters and smaller sections. The *Canon* consisted of around a million words in total. The first chapter dealt with human physiology, symptomatology and the main principles of diagnostic therapy. In chapter two, he provided an in-depth analysis of animal, vegetable and mineral types, highlighting the meaning, value and purpose of various minerals and herbs as cures for different ailments.

Chapter three focused on pathology, where Ibn Sina showed how to diagnose, treat and cure illnesses of different parts of the human body. In chapter four, he explained aspects of cosmetics, diseases related to hair, nails and obesity, and he showed how these ailments could be treated successfully. The fifth and last chapter of the book consisted of a large number of prescriptions in the form of tablets, pills, powders, syrup, herbs and various plant extracts. Ibn Sina's approach to medicine was rational as well as holistic because he explored the human body in its totality. That is to say, he believed it was important to consider both physiological and psychological factors for an effective treatment of illnesses. Uniquely, he even emphasised the importance of psychotherapy in combating certain types of illnesses and did so around nine hundred years before Sigmund Freud wrote on the subject.

Ibn Sina's *Canon* became so popular in the West that it was repeatedly translated into Greek, Latin and Hebrew between 1079 and 1608 CE. It was also used as a standard textbook at the universities of Paris, Montpellier and Louvain. The *Canon* was published in Europe more than thirty-five times during the sixteenth and seventeenth centuries. Interestingly, a recently discovered manuscript authored by Ibn Sina 'Treatise on Cardiac Drugs' and kept at Jamia Millia University library in New Delhi shows that he was not only an undisputed master and synthesiser of Greco-Islamic medicine, but also proves that he made remarkable and original contributions in the field of medicine in his own right.

If Ibn Sina was a great physician, then he must be considered one of the most distinguished philosophers of all time. Indeed, his *Kitab al-Shifa* is considered to be a philosophical masterpiece. It has four main topics, namely logic, physics, mathematics and metaphysics. In this encyclopaedic work, he provided a detailed explanation of his entire philosophy.

Neoplatonic is a philosophical system. As a Neoplatonist, Ibn Sina's philosophical views became highly controversial. He was influenced by the *ikhwan al-safa* (The Brethren of Purity), al-Farabi (see chapter 41) and others. He argued that the purpose of philosophy was to determine the true nature and reality of things to the best of one's ability. Thus, he believed that theoretical philosophy seeks the knowledge of the truth by perfecting the soul through the pursuit of knowledge alone, while practical philosophy seeks goodness through the adoption of knowledge of things that must be done.

As a philosopher, he was fiercely independent-minded and developed his views and thoughts on the subject, and also wrote freely on it. Though some of his ideas and thoughts concerning the nature of Allah, His Attributes and the concept of the eternity of the cosmos were considered heretical by his critics (such as al-Ghazali [see chapter 56], al-Shahrastani and Ibn Rushd [see chapter 60]), he was far from being an unbeliever.

Like his medical theories, Ibn Sina's philosophy became hugely influential both in the East and the West. Not surprisingly, his philosophical ideas and thoughts influenced some of the greatest thinkers of the Muslim world, including, al-Ghazali, Ibn Rushd, Suhrawardi (see chapter 64), al-Tusi (see chapter 68) and Mulla Sadra (see chapter 82). Likewise, influential Western thinkers like Albert the Great, William of Auvergne (b. 1190-d. 1249 CE), St. Thomas Aquinas (b. 1225-d. 1274 CE), Roger Bacon (b. 1220-d.

1292 CE) and Immanuel Kant (b, 1724-d. 1804 CE) were influenced by his philosophy and metaphysics.

Ibn Sina was familiar with the theological, philosophical and scientific ideas of his day. He was also familiar with the diversity of religious thought and interpretation which existed within the Muslim world at the time. He was born into an Isma'ili family;, his teacher Shaykh Isma'il al-Zahid was a Sunni jurist and theologian. He was also familiar with the *Ithna 'Ashari* (Twelver Shi'a) theology. Ibn Sina's awareness of these different Islamic groups and sects enabled him to engage in religious and philosophical discussions with scholars of all views.

Though it is not possible to say clearly whether he was a Sunni or Shi'a, there is no doubt that he considered himself to be a sincere Muslim. He respected both points of view. Ibn Sina fell ill and died on his way to Hamadan at the age of fifty-seven. He is known in the Muslim world as *shaykh al-rais* (the Chief of the Wise). His imposing portrait continues to grace the Great Hall of Paris University School of Medicine to this day, in recognition of his outstanding services to medicine and philosophy.

53

Ibn Hazm al-Andalusi
(b.994 - d.1064 CE) / (b.384 - d.457 AH)

The period from the eighth to the thirteenth century may have been a period of intellectual lack of progress in Europe, but it was not like that for the Muslims. It was the Golden Age of Islamic civilisation. It was a time when Muslim rule was high politically, economically and intellectually. From Makkah and Madinah to Baghdad, Damascus, Isfahan, Merv, Bukhara and Samarqand, Muslim greatness has very few examples to compare within world history. In less than fifty years after the death of the Prophet, Muslims reached North Africa and within a few more years they overpowered the Visigothic Kingdom of Iberia. *Al-Andalus* (or Islamic Spain) thus became a source of light for the rest of Europe. Under Islamic rule, Spain became a major centre of intellectual and literary activity. Cordova, the capital city of Muslim Spain, also boasted some of the finest colleges, libraries and hospitals in Europe.

When Islamic Spain reached its peak in the tenth century, under the stewardship of Caliph Abd al-Rahman III (see chapter 43), Cordova alone had more than seventy public libraries, containing more than half a million books on all the sciences of the day. But following the mass expulsion of Muslims from Spain by Ferdinand and Isabella in 1492 CE, Spain began to lose its former glory, to the extent that in the eighteenth century, there was not a single public library in Madrid. Yet, back in its glory days, Spain had produced some of Europe's most influential scholars and thinkers. One such scholar was Ibn Hazm al-Andalusi who was one of the great writers and thinkers of medieval Europe.

Ali ibn Ahmad ibn Sa'id ibn Hazm, known as Ibn Hazm al-Andalusi for short, was born in Cordova during the reign of Caliph Hisham II. Ibn Hazm traced his ancestors back to Yazid, an important Persian convert to Islam who lived during the early Umayyad period. According to the historian Ibn Hayyan, his ancestors, like his great-grandfather, Hazm, came from the town of Labla and were of Spanish descent. It was his grandfather, Sa'id, who first moved from Labla to Cordova where his family members became prominent scholars and politicians. It was in these roles that Ibn Hazm's father served both Caliph al-Hakam II (b. 915-d. 976 CE) and his successor Hisham II (b. 966-d. 1013 CE) as an advisor.

Ibn Hazm was educated at home by his learned father. He studied Arabic language, grammar, Qur'anic sciences and poetry as a child. Despite suffering from an irregular heartbeat from an early age – a medical condition which continued to trouble him all his life – he never allowed his health problems to hold him back. After completing his early education, he pursued advanced training in Islamic sciences under the guidance of Cordova's leading scholars. These included the traditionist al-Jasur, historian Ibn al-Faradi, and jurist Ibn Dahhun. He was keen to acquire expertise in philology, philosophy, logic, arithmetic and the natural sciences so he attended the lectures of Ibn Abd al-Warith, who was a prominent expert in local languages, and Ibn al-Kattani, who specialised in various scientific disciplines.

As a gifted student, Ibn Hazm was able to memorise and retain vast quantities of information. Impressed by his intellectual abilities, all his teachers predicted a bright future for the youngster. While he was still in his teens, he accompanied his father to conferences and official meetings and thus began to mix freely with Cordova's leading scholars and politicians. Rubbing shoulders with high-flying civil servants, outstanding literary figures and learned scholars made him confident and ambitious. He also became very aristocratic in his manners and etiquette. Unlike Caliphs Abd al-Rahman III and al-Hakam II, the reign of Hisham II was spoiled by considerable political instability and social disorder.

He was living during a politically unpredictable period in the history of Islamic Spain. So young Ibn Hazm was forced to undergo considerable personal suffering and hardship – especially after his father was humiliated and removed from his governmental post by his political rivals following Hisham II's abdication of power in 1010 CE. As the political situation rapidly deteriorated across Muslim Spain and ethnic conflict between the Arabs and the Berbers flared up, Ibn Hazm became actively involved in politics for the first time. In response, his opponents destroyed his family home in Balat Mughirah. He was imprisoned on more than one occasion. But, like his father, he remained loyal to the royal family and served them in the capacity of a Minister of State. It was a post that he held on three different occasions during the reigns of Caliphs Abd al-Rahman IV (d. 1018 CE), Abd al-Rahman ibn Hisham (b. 1001-d. 1024 CE) and al-Mu'tadd.

During this difficult period in the history of Islamic Spain, Ibn Hazm not only fulfilled his duties as a politician and advisor to successive Caliphs, but also found time for literary activities. As an extensive reader, he studied more books than probably any other scholar of his time. In doing so he gained mastery of a wide range of disciplines, including *ilm al-kalam* (speculative theology), *fiqh* (jurisprudence), *Hadith* (Prophetic traditions), history, comparative religion, logic and ethics. Indeed, the scope and scale of his learning was extremely massive. It was like an encyclopaedia. Despite being a busy politician and intellectual, he also found time to marry and start his own family. As it happens, Ibn Hazm's life can be divided into two parts. During the first period, he worked as a high-profile politician and administrator who tried to restore peace and security across Spain in the face of rising political conflict and ethnic tension.

This was by far the most hectic and uncertain period of his life and he experienced both the highs and lows of public position. Frustrated by the never-ending cycle of violence and political rivalry, he finally turned his back on public life at the age of about forty and entered a new phase where he focused all his time and energy on research and literary activities. He devoted the next thirty years of his life to the pursuit of knowledge, as well as writing books on a wide range of subjects including Islamic theology, jurisprudence, comparative religion, logic and ethics. This proved to be the most intellectually productive part of his life, for it was during this period that he authored some of his most influential works.

One such work was 'The Dove's Necklace concerning Love and Lovers'. It consisted of both prose and poetry. In this book, Ibn Hazm recorded his ideas about love and lovers. Although this was not the first book to be written on the subject in Arabic (as similar works already existed in that language), his insightful observations on the nature of love and human relationships made it a valuable contribution to the genre. A gifted psychologist and observer of human behaviour, he produced accurate psychological profiles of government officials, politicians and judges, as well as palace maids, by simply observing their behaviour and attitudes. According to Ibn Hazm, just as people often say one thing and do another, in the same way, the lovers promise each other much but do not always deliver.

In other words, his psychological observation of human behaviour revealed a natural contradiction between language, thought and action. That is why he argued that dishonesty and mistrust between lovers could be discovered by carefully observing their behaviour because language masks people's thoughts and emotions. Having spent his early years almost exclusively among women in his father's palace, he developed a powerful understanding of female psychology, as is evident from the perceptive comments he made about women's behaviour and attitude in his Dove's Necklace. He was fascinated by human behaviour and psychology, so he closely observed and recorded his views of different people, their behaviour and attitudes, and never ceased to revise and evaluate his understanding of moral theology and human psychology. He summed up his final thoughts on these subjects in his *Kitab al-Akhlaq wa'l Siyar* (The Book of Morality and Ethics).

His Dove's Necklace was first translated into English by A. R. Nyki of the Oriental Institute of Chicago in 1931 CE. The distinguished British Arabist A. J. Arberry published another translation in 1951 CE under the title of 'The Ring of the Dove'. 'The Book of Morality and Ethics' was translated by Muhammad Abu Layla of Al-Azhar Univerity in 1990 CE under the title of 'In Pursuit of Virtue: The Moral Theology and Psychology of Ibn Hazm Al-Andalusi'.

Ibn Hazm's other celebrated works include 'Judgement on the Fundamental Legal Principles' and 'The Decisive Treatise on Sects,

Heterodoxies and Denominations'. As an outstanding jurist, his books, he analysed and evaluated the fundamental sources and principles of *usul al-fiqh* (Islamic jurisprudence). He argued that all human actions can be classified into one of the five following juridical categories: *fard* (compulsory), *mustahhab* (commended), *makruh* (disliked), *haram* (outlawed) and *halal* (permissible). His systematic analysis of Islamic legal philosophy and method enabled Ibn Hazm to develop a set of complex grammatical and linguistic tools, which helped him to develop the *zahiri* legal method. Though the *zahiri* legal concepts were first proposed by Dawud al-Zahiri (b. 815-d. 883 CE) back in the ninth century, it was Ibn Hazm who, for the first time, provided a comprehensive description of *zahiri* legal principles.

Like the *Hanafi*, *Maliki* and *Shafi'i fuqaha*, he accepted the superiority of the Qur'an and *Sunnah* but, unlike them, he adopted an extremely literal interpretation of these two fundamental sources of *Sharia* (Islamic law). Thus, he deliberately focused on the *zahiri* (literal) – as opposed to the figurative or spiritual – interpretation of the scriptural sources. In addition, he rejected the validity of *qiyas* (analogical deduction), *istihsan* (personal welfare), *istislah* (community welfare) and *ra'y* (rational opinion) as sources of Islamic law. However, he considered *ijma* (collective consensus) to be a valid source of law so long as it was the *ijma* of the Prophet's *Sahabah* (companions), that is, the first generation of Muslims.

Perhaps Ibn Hazm's most influential work was his *Kitab al-Fasl*, which has been translated into Spanish. It consists of five large volumes in Arabic. This is a truly monumental work of scholarship and one of the first books to be written by a Muslim on comparative religion. He closely studied the thoughts of the early Muslim and non-Muslim philosophers and others. He was also familiar with the religious scriptures of Zoroastrianism, Judaism and Christianity. Moreover, he knew the Islamic theological debates of the Mu'tazilites, Ash'arites and others. So, in this book, Ibn Hazm provided a systematic and critical analysis of all the prevailing Islamic and non-Islamic philosophical, theological and mystical thoughts. Indeed, in his *Kitab al-Fasl*, he launched a ferocious intellectual assault on those philosophies, theologies and creeds he considered to be heretical and, in so doing, he attempted to discredit them one by one.

As a theologian, Ibn Hazm only believed in revelation and sensory data. Thus, he considered the *Kalam Allah* (Word of Allah) to be the most reliable and authoritative source of knowledge, along with human reason. Unlike some Muslim and non-Muslim philosophers, he emphasised the superiority of revelation over rationality. Indeed, he considered both revelation and reason to be complementary rather than contradictory. To be fair to Ibn Hazm, he also advocated the need for promoting tolerance and understanding between the world's great religions; as such, he was not only a pioneer of comparative religion but also a champion of inter-faith debate and dialogue.

If Ibn Hazm was a great religious thinker, then he must also be considered one of medieval Europe's most productive writers. According to his sons, Fadl and Abu Sulayman, the sheer quality and quantity of his works (consisting of more than four hundred books and essays, that is, around eighty thousand pages in total) proves that he was a scholar and writer of untiring energy. He achieved all this and more despite suffering from a catalogue of health problems, including irregular heartbeat, dry eyes and spleen abnormality. Far from being an intellectual who remained isolated, he played an active part in politics and public matters and also served as a Minister of State for three different Spanish Muslim rulers. However, unlike al-Zahrawi (see chapter 46), Ibn Tufayl (see chapter 58) and Ibn Rushd (see chapter 60), his works were not translated into Latin and therefore his ideas and thoughts did not gain much currency in the West.

By contrast, his works became popular in the Muslim world where they are rated very highly by students and scholars alike, thanks to the contributions of scholars like Ahmad Muhammad Shakir (b. 1892-d. 1958), Muhammad Abu Zahra (b. 1898-d. 1974), Sai'd al-Afghani (b. 1911-d. 1997 CE) and Ihsan Abbas (b. 1920-d. 2003 CE). Recently, European scholars have rediscovered the vast treasures of knowledge and wisdom he has left to future generations. Happily, many books and treatises are now available in various European languages on the life and thoughts of this great European Muslim writer and thinker. Ibn Hazm died in exile at the age of seventy and was buried in Niebla, located in the Spanish province of Seville. In recognition of his outstanding services to research and scholarship, in 1963 CE the Spanish authorities unveiled a life-size statue of this great Spanish Muslim thinker and writer.

Glossary

Imran Mogra

Alchemy – an ancient practice of recreating precious substances using recipes. Alchemists believed that materials like gold could be recreated with the right combination of ingredients.

Almagest – an astronomical manual by Ptolemy used by Muslim and European astronomers.

Aramaic – an ancient language, said to have been spoken by Jesus. It is used in the Talmud. It is sacred to Christians and Jews and used in religious rituals, texts and in public life too.

Austere – living with no luxuries, strict in manners, having a plain appearance. See *Zuhd*.

Bait al-hikmah – House of Wisdom, an Academy founded in 830 by Caliph Harun al-Rashid in Baghdad for the purpose of research, translation, teaching and learning.

Bedouins – nomadic Arabs living in the deserts of the Arabian Peninsula and across North Africa. The word Bedouin is from the Arabic word *'badawi'* meaning desert dweller. Most are animal herders, but many have abandoned their tribal traditions for urban lifestyles.

Bhagavad-Gita – lit. God's song; commonly known as the Gita. It is a dialogue recorded in the greatest poem of the Hindus. It is said to be 700 verses long. See *Mahabharata*.

Byzantine – The Byzantine Empire was a vast and powerful civilisation. It existed from 330 until it fell in 1453 CE to the Ottoman army who defeated Constantinople. It is often called the Eastern Roman Empire or simply Byzantium. Its capital was Constantinople (now Istanbul).

Caliph – in Arabic *Khalifah*, a successor of Prophet Muhammad who took responsibility and ruled on behalf of Allah and his messenger. The plural for *Khalifah* is *Khulafa*.

Creed – a set of systematic beliefs that influences the way a person lives, or a statement of faith.

Dervish – a member of a Ṣufi community or *tariqah*. Similar in meaning as the Arabic word *faqir* meaning those who depend upon Allah in everything they do, who chose material poverty and focus on rejecting the deceptions of ego (*nafs*) to reach Allah.

Euclid – a Greek mathematician who lived in Alexandria, Egypt around 300BCE. Often referred to as the Father of Geometry. He wrote the influential "Elements" - a comprehensive book of all the known mathematics of his time and the earliest known discussion of geometry. Fatimid – a dynasty of Muslim rulers in Egypt (10th - 12th century) who were descendants from Fatimah, the daughter of the Prophet.

Fiqh – lit. to understand; the study of Islamic law and jurisprudence. A specialist in Islamic law is a *faqih*, a scholar, sometimes called *Imam*. The plural is *fuqaha*.

Galen – a medical doctor (129-200 CE), his philosophy (Galenic thought) influenced the medieval period, a great intellectual of Western antiquity who wrote extensively.

Hasan – lit. good; a category of *hadith*. See *sahih, mawdu*.

Heretical – to belief or have a view which is against what is generally and normally accepted.

Herodotus – the ancient Greek historian (484 - 430/425 BCE).

Heterodoxy – these are beliefs and views different and against the accepted ones. See Orthodoxy.

Hijaz – meaning the barrier; the region of current Saudi Arabia. It is bordered in the west by the Red Sea, in the north by Jordan, in the east by the Najd and south by the Asir.

Hippocrates – the famous Greek physician (460 BCE - 375 BCE).

Ijma – the agreement of religious scholars about a legal judgement on an issue which is not directly ruled upon by the Qur'an and Sunnah. It is a collective consensus.

Ikhwan al-Safa – The Brotherhood of Purity, a secret society in Basra. It was forum for discussions, published the Treaties of The Brotherhood of Purity (*Rasa'il Ikhwan as- Safa*).

Ilm al-kalam – the study of Divine Speech, or speculative Islamic theology. *Kalam Allah* means the word and speech of Allah. See *kalam*.

Indus – Indus Valley area around one of the longest rivers (Indus), location of the world's first large civilisations around the area of modern-day Pakistan and Northern India.

Isnad – a chain of the names of all transmitters of a *hadith*. The names are carefully examined to check if it is a reliable report or not.

Istihsan – seeking good, community welfare, a legal principle used to establish a rule.

Jurisprudence – *fiqh*, law, Muslim legal system, there are four main schools (*madhhab*) of jurisprudence among the Sunni communities.

Jurist – an expert in law, a person trained in *fiqh* and *shari'ah*. See *faqih*.

Kalam – lit. speech; applied to Islamic theology which is the study of Divine Speech. These theologians were called *ahl al-kalam*, Imams or scholars of *kalam* or *mutakallimun*.

Khalifah – see Caliph.

Khawarij – meaning those exiting the community; the first sect of Islam, some of them believed that Muslims committing grave sins become disbelievers, known as *ghulat* (extremists), they opposed Ali and Muawiyah. Its singular is *khariji*.

Khwarizmshahs – an ancient title used regularly by the rulers of the Central Asian region until the arrival of the Mongols, after which it was used infrequently.

Lingua franca – a common language used for communication between different people who speak different languages.

Mahabharata – Indian epic poem of ancient India. See Bhagavad-Gita.

Mahdi – lit. the guided person; the one to appear before Qiyamah to return righteousness.

Manichaeism – is a dualistic religion founded by Mani in Babylonia in the 3rd century. He viewed himself as the last of prophets. It had mixed elements of Zoroastrianism, Buddhism, Christianity.

Mansur ibn Ishaq – Abu Salih, the Samanid governor of Rayy (d.915 CE).

Mantiq – lit. logic or speech; a science whose principles protect from making errors. It involves studying definitions and proofs. It enables accurate and clear thinking. It has three parts: conceptualisation, judgement and reasoning.

Manuscript – original copy of work before it is printed. It may be bound as a book, a scroll or consist of loose pages. Some are decorated with pictures, border decorations, embossed initial letters or full-page illustrations. Manuscript is abbreviated as MS.

Matn – this refers to the text of the *hadith* itself. It includes the actual words spoken by the Prophet Muhammad (ﷺ) as well as any commentary or context given by the narrator.

Mazdakism – a Magian priest in Persia who led a cult within Zoroastrian Mazdaeism. He preached that evil was equal to good. Light and darkness got mixed to create the world.

Medieval period – the period in Europe of expansion, centralisation and political disruption and violence, resulting in the foundation of many modern European countries. It was also dominated by a surge in Christianity by building cathedrals, clearing land by peasants, settling of new towns and villages, and building of great castles by local nobility. See Middle Ages.

Metaphysics – is a major work of Aristotle. In it he developed the doctrine of First Philosophy. It is one of the greatest philosophical works and its influence on the Greeks, the Muslims and other philosophers was huge.

Middle Ages – the period in European history between the fall of the Rome in 476 CE to the period of the Renaissance in the 13th, 14th, or 15th century.

Monism – the belief that all existence is one, there is only one thing and only one kind of thing.

Mutakallimun – *kalam* means speech. Theologians who study Divine Speech, justice, hell, and reject falsehood and defend Islam. See *kalam, Mu'tazila, Ashariyyah*.

Mystic – a person who follows a spiritual path or Sufi Order for self-purification. See Sufism.

Mysticism – the inner dimension, a path for spiritual knowledge and purity. See Sufism.

Neoplatonic – this is a philosophical system which started after Plato and is grounded in the teachings of Plotinus. It argued that this world is only a copy of an ideal reality which lies beyond this material world.

Orthodoxy – the generally accepted beliefs which do not depart from the original tradition. See heterodoxy.

Persia – This is ancient Iran. The term Persia was used for centuries, mainly in the West, to designate those regions where Persian language and culture dominated. The region of modern Iran. The Persian language is also known by Farsi or Parsi.

Philosophy – it is a form of rational and intellectual inquiry, it aims to be systematic, it tends to critically reflect on its own methods. The study of knowledge, reason, language and existence.

Qadi – usually a judge appointed by a ruler or a government on the basis of the extensive knowledge of Islamic law. The decision of a *qadi* is final.

Qiyas – analogical conclusion, a legal principle of working out new rulings for modern society by comparing these with the rules for similar situations already present in the Qur'an or Sunnah.

Rationalism – a school of thought which applied reason to the solutions of philosophical problems. See Mu'tazila.

Sahih – lit. correct, sound; usually refers to a *hadith* which is authentic. See Hasan.

Sanskrit – the ancient language in Hinduism. It was used as a means of communication by the Hindu Heavenly Gods. Sanskrit is also used in Jainism, Buddhism, and Sikhism. It is a complex language with vast vocabulary. It is used in reading sacred texts.

Semitic language – a language belonging to a subfamily of the Afro-Asiatic language family including Hebrew, Aramaic, Arabic, and Ethiopic. It covers a huge geographic region.

Socrates – founder (469-399 BCE) of Western philosophy. The best and the strangest Greek philosopher, questioned everything and everyone. His style of teaching is the Socratic method.

Sufi Order – a path of guidance to spiritual purification and character development to get closer to Allah and develop His love. There are many methods (Sufi Orders). See Naqshbandiyyah, Chishtiyah, Murabitun, Qadiriyah, Suhrawardiyya, Tijaniyya and others. See Sufism.

Sufism – in Arabic *Tasawwuf*, probably derived from *safa* meaning purity or *suf* meaning wool (simple garments). Sufism is often called Islamic mysticism or spirituality. It emphasises purification of the *nafs*, heart, mind, actions by developing piety, devotion, religiousness, *zikr*, and constant awareness of Allah. See Sufi, Sufi Order.

Tafsir – to explain and give commentary on the meaning of the verses of the Qur'an.

Tasawwuf – Islamic spirituality. See Sufism, Sufi, Sufi Order.

Teleological – the use of arguments to explain the existence of Allah in terms of the purpose they serve rather than of the cause. It relates to the belief of design and purpose in the world.

Theology – the study of the nature of Allah and religious beliefs from a religious point of view.

Transoxiana – included as the oldest states in Central Asia. It was located around the river Amu Darya (the River Oxus). Its territory varied depending on its ruler. It stretched into Afghanistan, eastern Iran, central Turkmenistan and parts of Kyrgyzstan, Uzbekistan and all of Tajikistan.

Vizier – a high-ranking political advisor or minister.

Zahiri – meaning literal and apparent; a school of law which adopts literally meanings as opposed to allegorical or mystical interpretation of texts. Now almost extinct.